LOST LINES

BRITISH NARROW GAUGE

NIGEL WELBOURN

Contents

First published 2000

ISBN 0 7110 2742 0

Published by Ian Allan Publishing

an imprint of Ian Allan Publishing Ltd, Terminal House, Shepperton, Surrey TW17 8AS.
Printed by Ian Allan Printing Ltd, Riverdene Business Park, Hersham, Surrey KT12 4RG.

Code: 0011/B1

Photographs
Front cover: courtesy Colour-Rail (2), Geoff Lumm (1)
Back Cover: courtesy Colour Rail (1), Geoff Lumm (2)

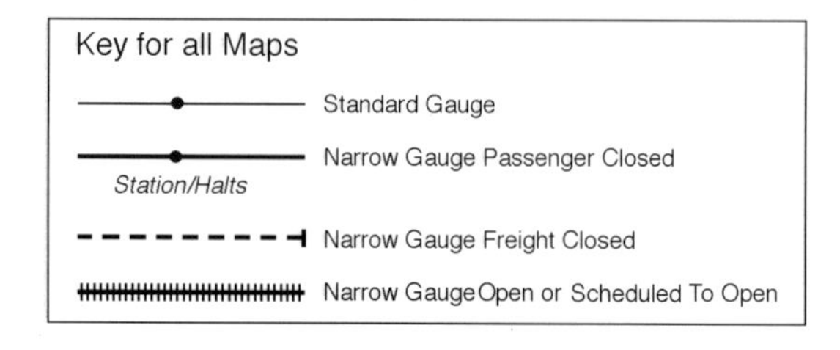

Introduction

In 1961, armed with Ian Allan's *abc Guide to Narrow Gauge Railways*, I first visited the narrow-gauge railways of Wales. I was enthralled by their unique charm and antiquity. At the age of 15, little could I have imagined that, almost four decades later, I would remain so captivated by this subject. I just hope that readers of this book will also be sufficiently enthused to visit some of the remaining narrow-gauge lines, as they rely on our support to keep going.

Unlike numerous lost main-line railways, many narrow-gauge lines were lightly built. In the course of researching this book I have been surprised by the lightness of some of the early rails and by the remoteness of some of the locations served. Yet an astonishing amount still remains, both physically along lines that have, in some cases, been closed for over 50 years, and with rolling stock that has found its way from closed lines to those that are open. Furthermore, lost narrow-gauge lines are remembered with great affection — so much so, that we should not rule out some of the lost lines described in this book being reopened.

Although this book is in a similar format to the other 'Lost Lines' volumes, narrow-gauge railways had mostly passed into history by the time the railways were nationalised and regionalised in 1948. As such, this volume is organised chronologically, based on the succession of public narrow-gauge line closures in Britain. In keeping with the series, a cross-section of lines and issues has been selected for historical interest. Consequently the Isle of Man, Jersey and Ireland receive attention. A number of industrial lines survived longest in their original form, and examples of the larger systems, some of which also ran private passenger services, are included in the final chapters.

Abbreviations

BR	British Railways
CDRJC	County Donegal Railways Joint Committee
GER	Great Eastern Railway
GNR(I)	Great Northern Railway (of Ireland)
GWR	Great Western Railway
LMS	London Midland & Scottish Railway
LMR	London Midland Region
LNER	London & North Eastern Railway
LNWR	London & North Western Railway
LSWR	London & South Western Railway
LYR	Lancashire & Yorkshire Railway
NER	North Eastern Railway
NRM	National Railway Museum
RAR	Royal Arsenal Railway
SR	Southern Railway
WD	War Department

Right: Enter a lost world. Rusting narrow-gauge tracks lead into the abandoned 730yd Moelwyn Tunnel on the Festiniog Railway (spelt historically with one 'f'). The southern portal is seen here on 22 August 1965. Opened in 1842, the tunnel last saw regular use in 1946. Although this section remains closed, a deviation allows today's Ffestiniog Railway once again to link Blaenau Ffestiniog and Porthmadog. *P. Plowman*

1 The battle of gauges

In the beginning, the gauge of a railway was not really important, as short individual sections of horse-worked tracks were not connected. At first, the scale and design of many railway wagons were similar to those of horse-drawn carts, and a considerable number of early mineral lines ended up being built to a gauge of just over 4ft. By way of example, the Tanfield Wagonway, Surrey Iron Railway and the Oystermouth Railway were all of about 4ft gauge. The 4ft 6in-gauge Lee Moor Tramway was one of a number of lines in the Dartmoor area built to a gauge only just below what was to become the British standard gauge, of 4ft 8½in. These lines (which are all now closed), although narrower than standard gauge, are probably better described as being of sub-standard, rather than true narrow gauge, which is often considered to be 3ft or less.

In North Wales, a number of lines were built to a nominal 2ft gauge. Narrower gauges had advantages, particularly over rugged terrain, in that they could turn sharper bends, thereby reducing earthworks, whilst the smaller loading gauge reduced the costs of construction and rolling-stock. The smaller gauge also allowed individual wagons to be manhandled. Speed was not a major consideration, as early lines had minerals as their main source of traffic, and competition from canals and horse-drawn road vehicles was limited.

As lines merged and longer journeys became possible, the issue of gauge became more important. Complaints grew about having to change trains on lines with different gauges, while the trans-shipment of goods became an increasing expense. Nevertheless, there was no unanimity over the most appropriate gauge. The Stephensons developed a successful network of lines in the North East at a gauge of 4ft 8½in. The Eastern Counties Railway was built to a 5ft gauge. Brunel favoured the broad 7ft gauge for the Great Western Railway.

A Royal Commission on Railway Gauges reported in 1846 and attempted standardisation at 4ft 8½in for all new railways, unless otherwise specified. The Act that followed spelt the end of the broad, 7ft gauge of the Great Western Railway, but it did not prevent narrow-gauge lines from being built, or attempt to stipulate any preferred width of narrow gauge.

There was little consensus about the most appropriate narrow gauge. In some cases existing rolling stock dictated the gauge, but new lines were built to a bewildering variety of differing narrow gauges. The first metre-gauge line between Crich and Ambergate opened in 1841. The success of the Festiniog Railway convinced many of the virtues of a 2ft gauge. The vast Woolwich Arsenal system developed using a 1ft 6in gauge, while Sir Arthur Heywood demonstrated that even a 'minimum gauge'

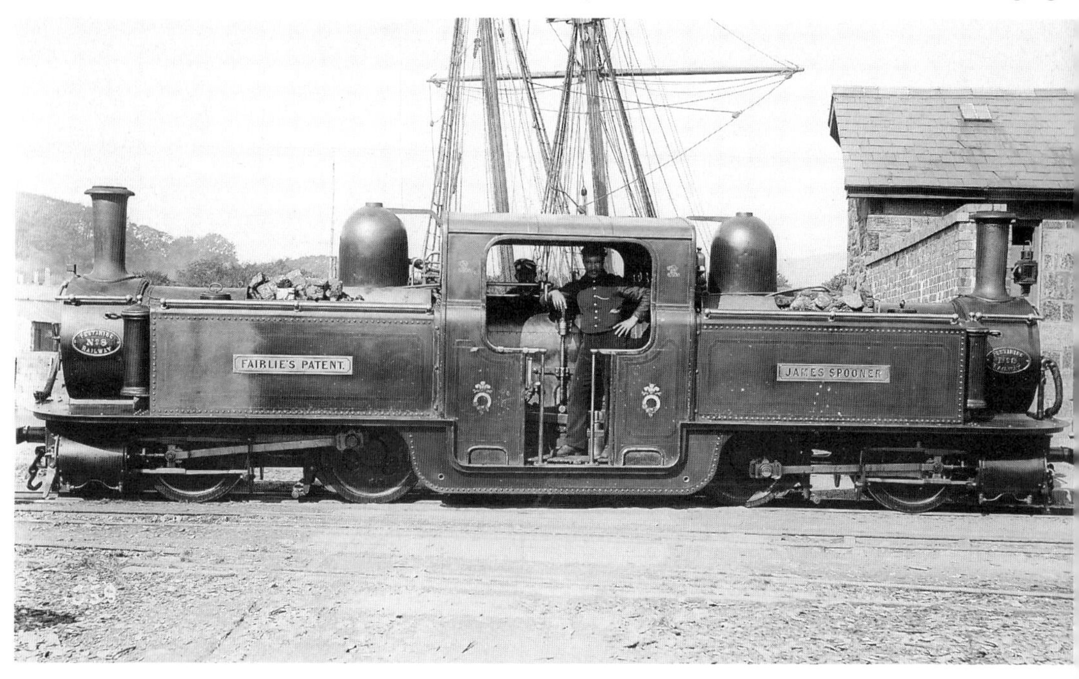

Above: The first narrow-gauge lines developed from the need to convey heavy minerals, in particular coal. Early mineral tramways can be traced back to the 1600s, and were of assorted gauges. Here, narrow-gauge track is seen emerging from an original drift coalmine, preserved at the Beamish Museum in the North of England, in September 1999. *Author*

Below left: Superpower on the 1ft 11½in-gauge Festiniog Railway. Fairlie's double engine *James Spooner*, named here after the great narrow-gauge engineer, is seen at Portmadoc quayside in the early 1900s. The articulated engine could haul more than twice the load of a conventional engine. The sailing ship behind the locomotive recalls the days when Welsh slate was exported to all parts of the world.
Locomotive Publishing Co

Above: The transport of minerals was the *raison d'être* of most narrow-gauge railways, and some were to survive for many years efficiently carrying out this function. This view, taken in 1954, is of slate trucks on a horse-operated section of the 2ft 3in-gauge Corris Railway, at the Aberllefeni Quarries in Wales. *M. Ware*

Below: Andrew Barclay's Kilmarnock works, with six 0-4-0 well-tank locomotives being constructed for 2ft narrow-gauge railway use. Intended for industrial use on rough track, the strongly-built engines were similar in appearance to those built by Orenstein & Koppel of Berlin. In 1918 six locomotives of this design were under construction for the Air Service Construction Corps. *Ian Allan Library*

Left: Nantmor on the 1ft 11½in-gauge Welsh Highland Railway, on the section of line that threads its way through the rocks towards the Aberglaslyn Pass. Narrow-gauge construction was well suited for remote and rugged country, such as North Wales, as sharper curves and a narrower loading gauge enabled construction costs to be reduced. *Ian Allan Library*

Below: With the exception of Glasgow's underground and some pleasure lines, Scotland's only public narrow-gauge passenger railway was the 2ft 3in-gauge Campbeltown & Machrihanish Light Railway, on the Kintyre peninsula. Here a train waits for a Clyde steamer connection on the quayside at Campbeltown, prior to the railway's closure. *SLS*

railway of 1ft 3in could successfully transport freight on his estate. Today, a railway of 15in gauge or narrower, if operated by scale model locomotives, is generally considered to be miniature gauge.

Up until 1864 it had been forbidden to construct narrow-gauge lines for public passenger use. Charles Spooner, of the Festiniog Railway (spelt historically in the Act with one 'f'), pioneered steam use on this line in 1863. He also began to carry passengers, pending the outcome of an application to the Board of Trade to formalise this. In 1865 history was made when approval was given to run the first public passenger services on a narrow-gauge line.

Other lines also introduced passenger services for workers and local people. Those lines built on private land considered that they needed no statutory permission. Others, not on private land, took out powers to convey passengers. In some cases, services were not on a regular basis, while on many lines passenger coaches were mixed in with freight trains.

In 1873 a narrow-gauge (3ft) system was opened on the Isle of Man, and passengers were a primary consideration from the start. The Isle of Man Railway, as with many island railways, was never likely to be connected with the mainland and could choose a gauge most suited to Manx needs. The 3ft gauge was also adopted for secondary railways in Ireland, and was considered by many at this time to provide an optimum balance between economy of construction and flexibility of operation.

Although not the subject of this book, narrow-gauge street and pier tramways were also primarily built for passengers. They were established throughout Britain and ranged from the remote Pwllheli & Llanbedrog Tramway, which ran on the coast in North Wales until closed by storm damage,

Above: In 1929 a standard-gauge line was laid from Ravenglass to Murthwaite. The difference between the 15in gauge of the Ravenglass & Eskdale Railway and the BR standard 4ft 8½in-gauge line is apparent in this view of the shared right of way, taken at Murthwaite, in May 1950. *H. C. Casserley*

Below: Narrow-gauge lines reached the parts other railways could not, and were to be found in the most obscure and remote locations. In this view, a petrol tractor hauls a coach onto a grouse moor on the 2½-mile-long, 2ft 6in-gauge Dalmunzie House Hotel Railway, before the closure of the Scottish hotel, in 1978. *T. Rindlay*

Nº
6

759
SOUTHERN
188
SOUTHERN

Left: A number of narrow-gauge secondary passenger lines were built in Ireland, all to a 3ft gauge. Here No 6, a mighty 4-8-4T of the Londonderry & Lough Swilly Railway, is seen in 1931. It heads an eight-coach train at Buncrana, on the 30-mile line from Londonderry to Carndonagh. *Real Photographs*

Below left: A double-headed train on the 1ft 11½in-gauge Lynton & Barnstaple Railway. The heavily-graded line was the longest of the English narrow-gauge passenger lines and was well used during the summer peak periods. Here, in Southern Railway livery, No 188 *Lew* and No 759 *Yeo* are seen at Pilton on Sunday 29 September 1935 — the last day of services on the line. *Ian Allan Library*

Below: Isle of Man Railway Beyer Peacock 2-4-0T No 5 *Mona*, dating from 1874, passes a derelict signal near Braddan Bridge with an evening special on the now-closed line from Douglas to Peel. An extensive 3ft-gauge passenger system developed on the Isle of Man, and fortunately parts still survive. *A. Stewart*

to the extensive urban systems that once existed in the West Midlands.

The Light Railways Act of 1896 gave impetus to the development of lightly-constructed narrow-gauge lines in rural areas. The Act allowed relaxation of the usual Board of Trade requirements in respect of level-crossing gates and other equipment, thus reducing costs, although safety considerations required speeds to be limited to 25mph. The Leek & Manifold, Vale of Rheidol, Welshpool & Llanfair and Campbeltown & Machrihanish light railways were among those which took advantage of the Act. All were of narrow gauge, but mostly of differing gauges.

Many other narrow-gauge lines were proposed, but few were completed, schemes being either abandoned or built to standard gauge. The last significant public narrow-gauge line to open in Britain was the Ashover Light Railway, in Derbyshire, in 1924. Even as it was being constructed, the era of narrow-gauge railways was drawing to a close; standard gauge had won the battle of gauges.

2 To the edge of extinction

As the main-line railway network grew, narrow-gauge lines were few and far between. Although narrow-gauge railways could be found on the top of Snowdon and in the deepest colliery, in the 1920s there were only about 50 miles of public narrow-gauge line operating in England. Standard-gauge light railways could often cover the terrain at little additional cost, and trans-shipment difficulties were avoided. Those narrow-gauge lines that had been built involved the transfer of goods between gauges. As motor transport became more reliable and economic, short sections of narrow-gauge line became increasingly vulnerable and uneconomic. An omen of the future came with the closure of the Ravenglass & Eskdale Railway in 1913.

Lines that continued to run were forced to make economies to survive. In 1924 Colonel Stephens was appointed chairman of the Festiniog and Welsh Highland railways. He also had involvement in other narrow-gauge lines, including those at Rye, Snailbeach and Ashover. From a house in Tonbridge, he applied his skills to the economic running of such lines, yet even his ingenuity was unable, in the end, to ensure the survival of the railways concerned.

The closure of the Southwold Railway in 1929 came as a shock. The loss of the Lynton & Barnstaple Railway in 1935 attracted genuine sadness. Soon, even the famous Festiniog Railway was fighting for its life. World War 2 was the death-knell for most remaining lines and saw the end of most regular passenger services. Few expected those narrow-gauge lines that survived the war to continue for much longer.

The Great Western Railway had lost little time in closing passenger services on the Corris and Welshpool & Llanfair lines. Yet the GWR was equally active in reopening the scenic Vale of Rheidol Railway for summer tourists, in 1945. Sadly the Festiniog Railway had not the resources to continue, and closed the following year.

Nationalisation would not save the Corris line, which was closed by British Railways in 1948, and a similar fate awaited the Welshpool & Llanfair line in 1956. It seemed that the few remaining independent lines, such as the Talyllyn, would soon also close. In Ireland, a number of lines continued to operate, but, even where new rolling stock was provided, other infrastructure was in an ever-deteriorating condition.

The outlook looked very bleak, most remaining lines having seen little investment. They were simply worn out and in an advanced state of decline and retrenchment. By their very nature, they generally served remote and isolated communities. Even in their heyday, many were often at the margins of profitability, eking out a living where standard-gauge lines would not have been viable. There were no great reserves of cash, and damage by fire, flood or warfare led to closures. British narrow-gauge lines could well have been confined to the history books.

In 1950 Sir Henry Haydn Jones died. He had made every effort to keep the Talyllyn Railway open, but on his death it was clear that services would cease. At this low-point, volunteers, led by Tom Rolt, stepped in and saved the Talyllyn Railway from certain death, and the world's first railway preservation society to save a narrow-gauge railway was set up.

The Talyllyn Railway had shown just what could be done, inspiring others to give their time, energy and money, and a fightback ensued elsewhere. Consequently, after years of unremitting decline, there came a turning point. Against all the odds, a number of narrow-gauge lines have come back from the very edge of extinction to form a well-known part of Britain's railway heritage.

Left: The first narrow-gauge line to succumb to bus competition was the Southwold Railway, in April 1929. There was no real precedent for dealing with such events, and on closure the stock simply rotted on the track in anticipation of reopening. Here, derelict carriages are seen at Halesworth in 1939.
Ian Allan Library

Right: The Saundersfoot Railway & Harbour opened in 1832 and the 4ft-gauge line linked anthracite collieries with the harbour at Saundersfoot, near Tenby. This view of the disused coastal section was taken in July 1938, and remaining sections of the line closed the following year. Parts of the route are now used as a coastal footpath. *S. Oborne*

Centre right: A view on the Festiniog Railway above Tan-y-Bwlch, showing the typical mountain terrain through which the line runs. This view of the 60yd Garnedd Tunnel was taken in September 1960, prior to the reopening of this section of line. Today, tree cover in the Vale of Ffestiniog has softened the landscape in this area. *R. Roberts*

Below right: Exposed to the weather and vandals since the line closed in 1946, derelict stock is seen here rotting away at Portmadoc station in the summer of 1953. The Festiniog Railway applied for an abandonment order in 1950; fortunately the Ministry of Transport refused and the line was later brought back from the very edge of extinction. *M. Ware*

Left: The decline of the Welsh slate industry resulted in the loss of all the major narrow-gauge slate lines. Here, a forlorn row of derelict engines, including a De Winton (just visible), a Manning Wardle and a Bagnall, are seen at Bethesda on the Penrhyn Railway in 1956. *N. Gurley*

Centre left: A derelict signal near Whitegates crossing, looking towards Lee Moor, on the 4ft 6in-gauge Lee Moor Tramway. The mineral railway was last regularly used in 1939, but infrastructure remained intact and use of the lower part of the line continued until 1960. *Ian Allan Library*

Below left: The Eastwell iron ore quarries operated a 3ft-gauge system. Here, Avonside-built 0-6-0T *Nancy* is seen in July 1961, awaiting disposal following the line's closure in 1959. The locomotive, dating from 1908, was originally used on the short Brewer's Grave Tramway. *G. King*

Above right: The Groudle Glen Railway, with a Bagnall 2-4-0T, *Sea Lion*, dating from 1896, seen here in a derelict condition behind the locomotive shed on 9 September 1961. The 2ft-gauge railway was cut back after World War 2, and only the more inquisitive visitors to the Isle of Man could find the truncated remains. The line closed in 1962, but this was not to be the end of the railway, or its locomotives. *Ian Allan Library*

Far right: A neglected — but not lost — Abergynolwyn station on the Talyllyn Railway. A mineral extension ran on to the foot of the Alltwyllt incline, and a further incline allowed wagons of coal and supplies to be lowered into Abergynolwyn itself. Such ingenuity was not to save the line, but such evocative views of the narrow-gauge railway were to help inspire enthusiasts mount a pioneering rescue. *Locomotive Publishing Co*

Right: Ex-Donegal Railway 4-6-4T *Erne*, built by Nasmyth Wilson in 1904. It is seen here stranded at Letterkenny on 11 June 1965, after being used for track-lifting on the closure of the railway in 1960. Purchased for preservation in the USA, trans-shipment costs proved prohibitive and, following a period of dereliction, the locomotive was sadly scrapped in 1967. *C. Prout*

USA

3 'Owd Ratty'

In 1913, without any great ado, the Ravenglass & Eskdale Railway became the first significant and long-established public narrow-gauge passenger railway to close. Now known as the 'Owd Ratty', the railway had been the first narrow-gauge line in England to offer a public passenger service. Fortunately, most of its route, running deep into the wilds of the Lakeland fells, is still in use, as today's miniature railway runs along much of the trackbed of the earlier narrow-gauge line.

The original 3ft-gauge line was built for the Whitehaven Mining Co, to connect its haematite iron mines in Eskdale with the Furness Railway at Ravenglass. A link to the port at Ravenglass was proposed, but never constructed. The 7¼-mile line opened to freight in May 1875 and, after many improvements, to passengers in November the following year.

The railway was never particularly profitable, and soon the Whitehaven Mining Co went bankrupt; as a consequence, the Ravenglass & Eskdale Railway was set up to run the line. The Gill Force Mine line closed, but the railway survived on general goods and weekend tourists. On a few busy occasions, passengers were forced to ride in open trucks on 'the route to the Alps', as adverts proclaimed it. Nevertheless, outside the main holiday periods there was little passenger traffic. The remaining line ran on a make-do-and-mend basis until 1908, when complaints about the parlous state of the track led to passenger services being suspended in November of that year.

In 1910 a new Eskdale Railway planned to electrify the line, but could not raise sufficient finance. Freight continued on an occasional basis until 1912, when the mines flooded, and the last train ran in April 1913. For a while, much of the stock remained rusting on the track, but the two locomotives, *Devon* and *Nab Gill* (or *Nabb Gill*, as evidence now suggests), were scrapped in 1915.

Narrow Gauge Railways Ltd, a subsidiary of Bassett-Lowke Ltd, was formed by a group of enthusiasts to inject new life into the 'Owd Ratty'. In 1915 they took over the derelict 3ft line to create a new 15in-gauge miniature railway. (At the same time, they

Below: Nabb Gill, a Manning Wardle 0-6-0T dating from 1874, and a single coach are seen here at Boot, during the early days of the 3ft-gauge line. The locomotive was out of use from 1908 and was scrapped in 1915. *SLS*

effected a similar transformation on the former 2ft-gauge horse-operated Fairbourne Railway in Wales.) The new line utilised much of the old track and sleepers, opening to Muncaster Mill in 1915 and to Boot by 1917. It also used some stock from the Duffield Bank system, after the death of the latter's owner, Sir Arthur Heywood, in 1916.

The section of line between Boot and Dalegarth was soon closed, due to the steep gradient leading to Boot station. Meanwhile, in the 1930s, granite quarries provided new freight for the line, with trains running to a crushing plant at Murthwaite. A section of mixed-gauge track was also provided from the plant to Ravenglass. Passenger services were discontinued during World War 2, but recommenced in 1946.

The Beckfoot quarry was closed in 1953, and attempts to sell the line were unsuccessful. Consequently, in 1960, the line was put up for public auction, with the possibility of its being sold in 60 lots and becoming a 'lost line'. A campaign to save the railway was mounted and a preservation society established. This was a success, and happily the 'Ratty', running between Ravenglass and Eskdale, remains open today.

Above: Devon, a Manning Wardle 0-6-0T also dating from 1874, and seen here hauling a rickety collection of coaches and a covered van at Eskdale Green. *Devon* hauled the first freight train over the line in May 1875. In 1905 the locomotive was derailed and toppled onto its side near Murthwaite. It was recovered to run again, but was scrapped a decade later. *Bucknall Collection*

Right: A short freight train of two wagons and a van, hauled by *Nabb Gill*, running at the turn of the last century. The driver wears a large white hat. The fencing appears to be in as poor a condition as the track. The latter became so rough that passenger services were withdrawn in November 1908 on the instructions of Winston Churchill, then President of the Board of Trade. *Bucknall Collection*

Above: A single-coach narrow-gauge train heading towards Ravenglass, at Beckfoot station, with the Stanley Ghyll Hotel in the background. The hotel and subsequent miniature railway remain, although a number of mature trees have grown up between the railway and the hotel since this view was taken about a century ago. *SLS*

Left: The four-wheeled 'Big Saloon' was also used to convey passengers. The unusual vehicle can be seen here standing partly under the overall roof of the original Ravenglass narrow-gauge passenger station. *Ian Allan Library*

Below left: Ravenglass, with the original wooden passenger station building and overall platform roof, together with some of the former 3ft-gauge rolling stock. The Furness Railway main-line signalbox can just be made out in the background, to the right of the narrow-gauge station. *Locomotive Publishing Co*

Right: A banner in the museum at Ravenglass heralds the reopening of the Eskdale Railway in 1915 as a 15in-gauge line. By August 1915 miniature trains were running as far as Muncaster Mill, and two years later re-gauging had reached Boot. *Author's collection*

Below: The reopening as a 15in-gauge railway in 1915 created considerable interest. This view shows *Sans Pareil* and rolling stock from Sir Arthur Heywood's Eaton Hall system at Ravenglass. The old wooden station structure, seen in the background, was demolished in 1928. The uneven tracks in the foreground are the remains of the earlier 3ft-gauge railway. *Ian Allan Library*

Right: Part of the closed original line to Boot. A short section of 3ft-gauge track has been relaid on this bridge, as this view looking towards Boot in September 1999 shows. 3ft-gauge passenger trains last used the line in 1908. *Author*

Left: The remains of Boot station. The passenger facilities have long since gone, but the derelict remains of the haematite-iron-extraction industry can still be found in the area. At one time an incline to ore workings operated from the station. This view dates from September 1999. *Author*

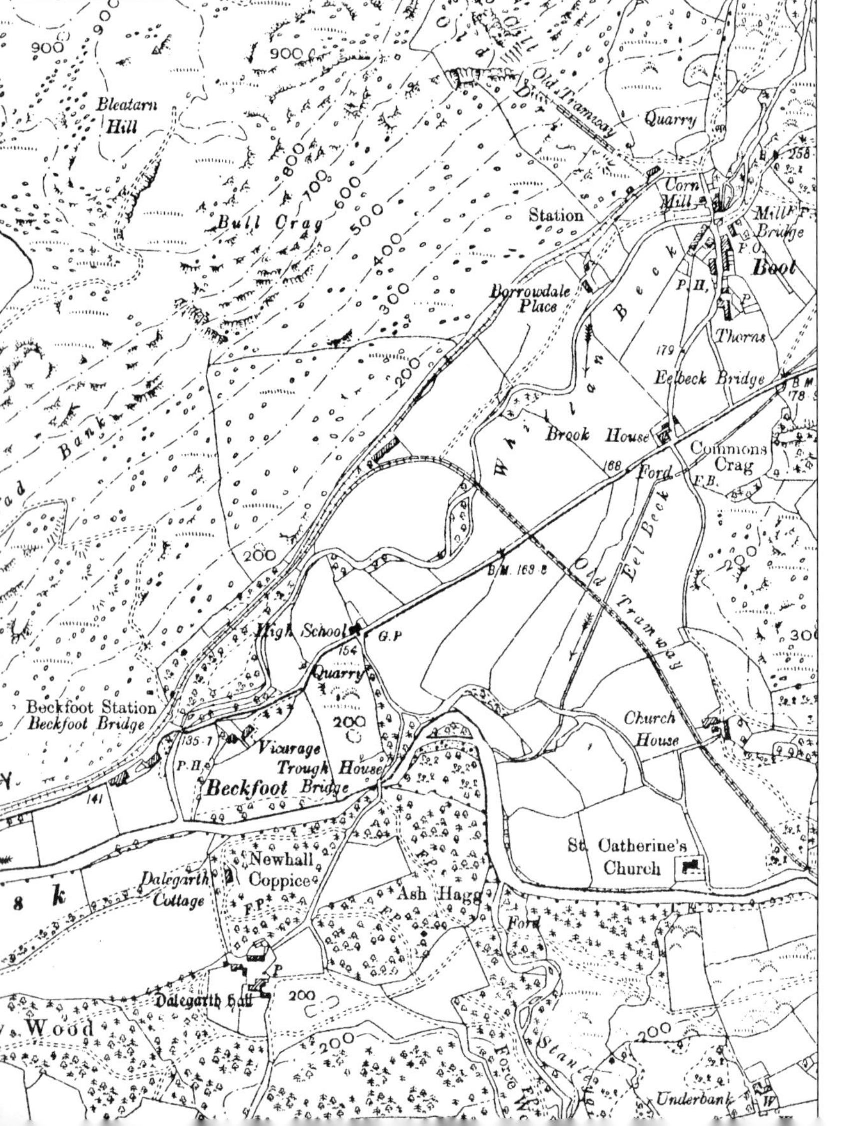

Below left: Map showing the original 3ft-gauge route to Boot and the 'Old Tramway' to the Gill Force mine running to the southeast, in 1900. The current miniature line was cut back from Boot, owing to the steep gradients; in 1926 it was extended to the terminus at Eskdale (Dalegarth), which is located on the 'Old Tramway' to Gill Force. *Crown copyright*

Right: A mixed train passes through the fir trees of the Heronry, on the attractive section of line between Wenhaston and Southwold, during the mid years of the railway's operation. The line was one of just three public 3ft-gauge lines in England. *Bucknall Collection*

4 Southwold — service suspended

The next major closure was that of the Southwold Railway, in 1929.

During the 19th century, as the national railway network developed and coastal holiday resorts became more popular, Southwold had become one of the few towns of any size on the east coast not to be served by a railway. Consequently, various schemes were put forward to connect it with the main East Suffolk line.

Following consideration of the anticipated traffic and after sufficient finance was eventually raised, an 8¾-mile-long, 3ft narrow-gauge line was decided upon, running from Halesworth to the coast. The line was opened in September 1879 and, although it was built to a narrow gauge, the likelihood of future conversion to standard gauge was not ruled out.

A 1-mile branch was built to the port at Southwold in 1914, but by this time World War 1 had put an end to the coastal fishing industry (see *Lost Lines — Eastern*). Nevertheless, after World War 1 summer passenger traffic increased. As a result, plans to convert the railway to standard gauge went ahead, with some bridges and structures being widened in anticipation.

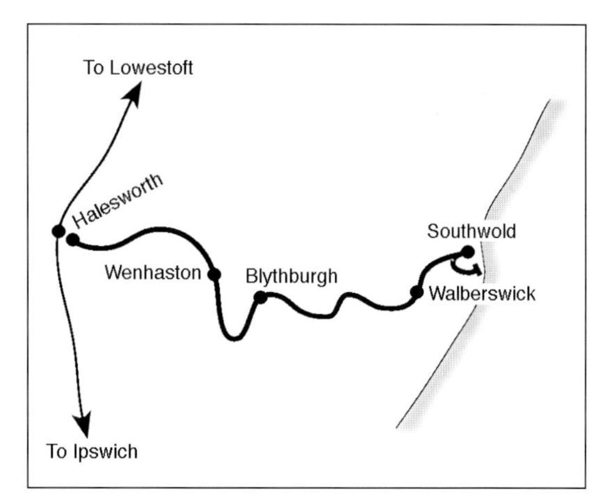

The railway had great character and the route to the coast via Blythburgh church, the Heronry and over the River Blyth swing bridge was most appealing. The locomotives were also particularly attractive and named after features and settlements along the route. They were none too powerful, but as speed was limited to 16mph this was not a major problem.

The need for the trans-shipment of goods, and bus competition — including a direct service from Southwold to Lowestoft — soon began to cut into the railway's profits. The line remained independent at the grouping in 1923, but in 1926 the first loss (of £4) was recorded. In 1927 the railway again made a profit, but it was to be the last.

Efforts were made in an attempt to ensure the line's survival. Staff were forced to take pay cuts, services were increased to compete with buses, and fares were reduced. However, from 1928, buses were allowed to pick up passengers anywhere in Southwold and even the staff pay cut of 1928 could not prevent growing anxieties about the financial state of the railway. There were no great cash reserves, and consequently, in 1929, the railway appealed for help to Southwold Corporation and to the LNER. Both refused to assist and as a consequence, in an action now largely acknowledged as rash, the line was closed in April 1929 and the 30 members of staff were made redundant.

This was the first independent public narrow-gauge passenger line of significance to succumb to road competition. At the time, it was fondly believed that help with some sort of reopening, if only for freight, would follow. Yet plans for reopening were not well co-ordinated, and all attempts at revival failed. The route remained in a moribund state until World War 2, when the swing bridge over the River Blyth was blown up to hinder any possible invasion. In 1941 a start was made on scrapping the remaining stock, and the track was cut up to aid the war effort.

The prospect of reopening was made ever more difficult, although attempts have continued sporadically. In the 1960s the railway company was finally wound up, but there were some interesting remains at that time. These included the station buildings at Southwold and a footbridge over the cutting on Southwold Common, although both would soon be demolished.

Even today, one of the chestnut trees planted at Southwold station remains and a Bailey bridge uses the footings of the original swing bridge over the River Blyth. Parts of the route are used as footpaths and a short section of track remains on the harbour branch. An original covered van can be found at the East Anglia Transport Museum at Carlton Colville, and small exhibits, including lamps, station bells and tickets, in the Southwold Museum. There is a Southwold Railway Society, with aims to reinstate a section of the line.

SOUTHWOLD and HALESWORTH (1st and 3rd class).—Southwold.
Secretary, H. Ward. Chairman, A. C. Pain.

Miles	Up.	Week Days. mrn	mrn	aft	aft	aft (Saturdays only.)
	Southwold ....dep.	7 30	1055	2 20	5 25	7 10
1	Walberswick ......[ford	7 33	1058	2 23	5 28	7 13
4	Blythburgh, for Wang-	7 45	1110	2 35	5 40	7 25
6½	Wenhaston	7 56	1121	2 46	5 51	7 36
9	Halesworth 288, 292 ar	8 7	1132	2 57	6 2	7 47
9¾	292 London (L'pool St.) a	11½n	3 30	6 0	9 25	....

Miles	Down.	Week Days. mrn	mrn	mrn	aft	aft (Saturdays only.)
	Liverpool Street, 288 London ....dep.	5 5	10 0	1145	3 25	5 0
—	Halesworth ......dep.	8 40	1 12	3 20	6 23	7 53
2½	Wenhaston.... ..[ford	8 49	1 21	3 29	6 32	8 2
5	Blythburgh, for Wang-	9 0	1 32	3 40	6 43	8 13
8	Walberswick	9 14	1 46	3 54	6 57	8 27
9	Southwold ....arr.	9 17	1 49	3 57	7 0	8 30

n Arrives at 10 45 mrn. on Mondays.

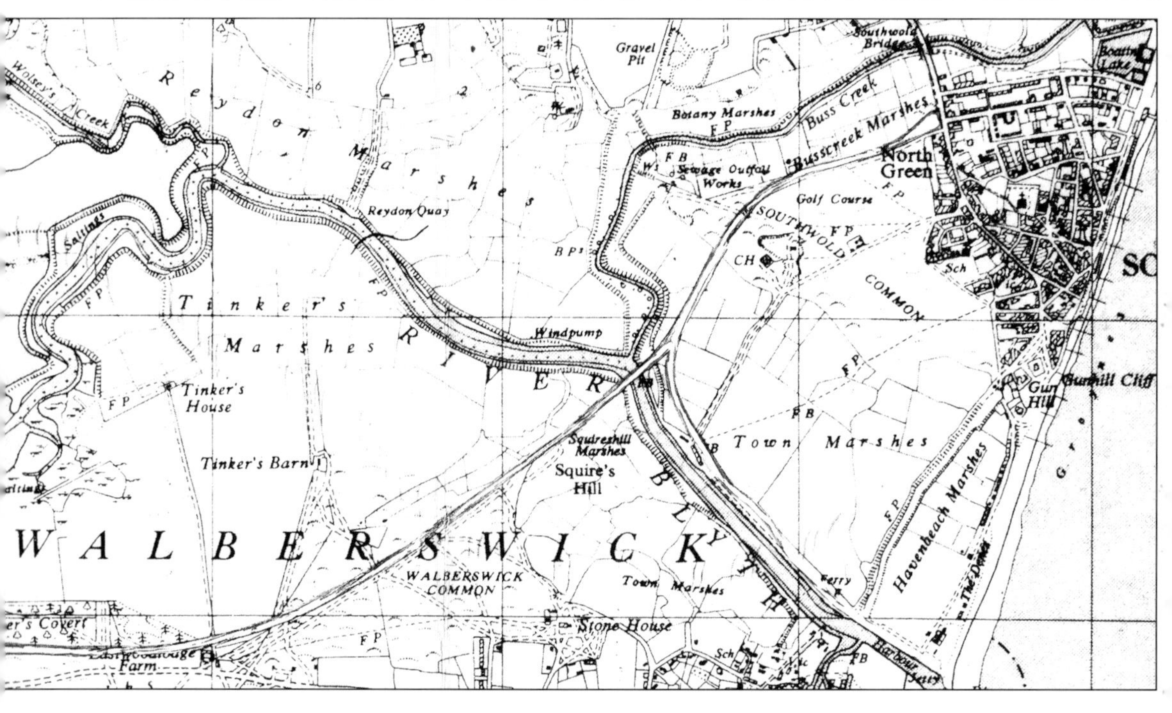

Right: No 1 *Southwold*, a 2-4-2T, was purchased from Sharp Stewart in 1893. The original No 1 was returned to its builder because of financial difficulties. The locomotive in this view is getting up steam at Southwold shed in about 1910. The engine required heavy repairs in 1928 and was withdrawn from service. It was the first locomotive to be scrapped, in 1929, after closure of the line. *LPC*

Centre right: No 3 *Blyth*, an attractive Sharp Stewart 2-4-0T, was hired by the railway before being purchased in 1890. It is seen here at Southwold prior to World War 1. A new boiler was provided for the engine in 1925. On closure of the railway, in 1929, the locomotive rusted in Halesworth engine shed for 12 years, before being scrapped in 1942.
Ian Allan Library

Below right: A view from the 1960s, from the town side, of the former booking office at Southwold station. The building lingered on after closure in an increasingly dilapidated and sorry state. A covered van once used on the line was sited on the former station toilet area at this time; the station was finally demolished in 1968. Today the site has been redeveloped, but one of the horse chestnut trees planted on the platform still remains.
David Lawrence

SOUTHWOLD (Suffolk).
Station closed. See trains to Halesworth and thence by Road Motor

Above left & above: Passenger services in 1910 and 1930.

Left: The disused railway track in the Southwold area in the 1950s.
Crown copyright

G. E. R.

om

TO

SOUTHWOLD

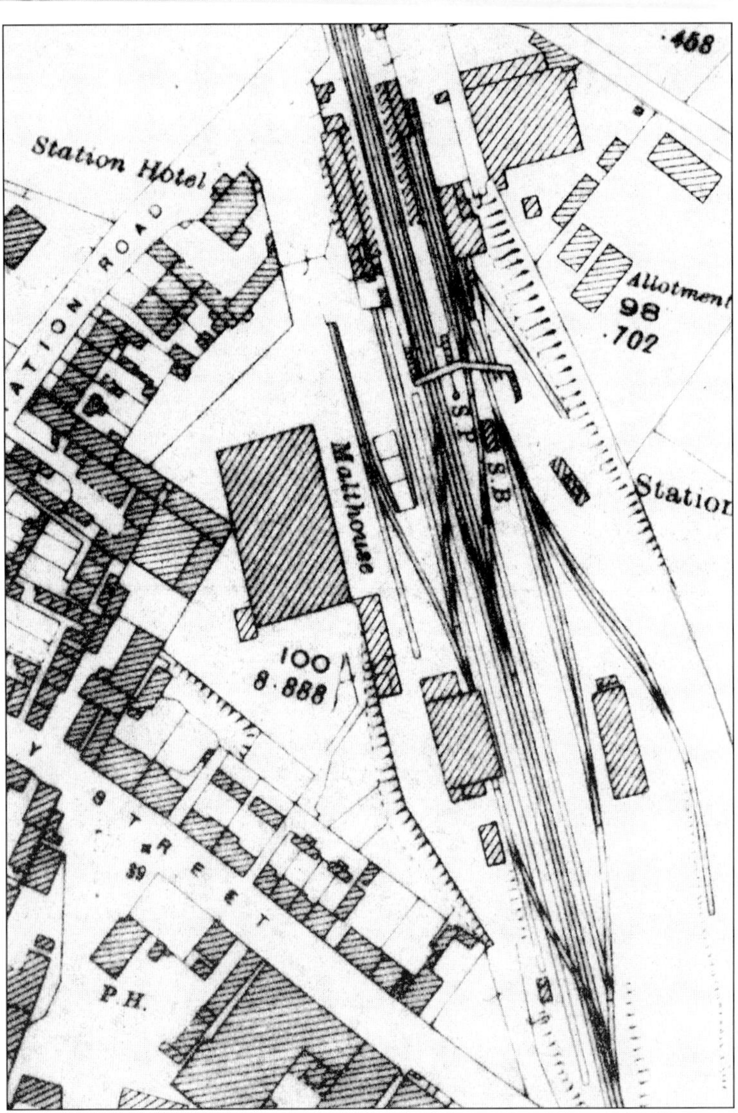

Left: Halesworth station yard, with carriage No 6 in a derelict condition, in 1939. The railway owned six coaches; the livery seen here was a dull red with white lettering. The coaches were fitted with Cleminson's flexible-wheelbase system, an idea designed to make six wheels do the work of two bogies. *Ian Allan Library*

Above right: Halesworth station yard, with abandoned wagons and overgrown track, in 1939. The wagon fleet consisted of 39 vehicles. Stock was mainly four-wheeled, although Thomas Moy Ltd owned a number of six-wheeled coal wagons. The outbreak of World War 2 was to lead to scrapping of the remaining stock.
Ian Allan Library

Centre right: The elegant and slender footbridge at Southwold Common in the 1950s. It was built after the line was opened with old rails, and Southwold Golf Club paid £50 for its construction. In the 1960s the structure became unsafe. None other than the Town Clerk cut the bridge down, in a cost-saving exercise. *David Lawrence*

Below right: A similar view of Southwold Common in June 1999. This was the only cutting of any consequence on the railway. The concrete foundations of the footbridge remain. The gorse and vegetation generally has grown considerably since the 1950s and the railway is now used as a footpath. *Author*

Left: The station yard at Halesworth in the 1950s. The standard-gauge interchange siding remained long after closure and removal of the narrow-gauge track.
Crown copyright

Above: The Bailey bridge over the River Blyth, between Southwold and Walberswick, is seen here in June 1999. The footbridge uses some of the footings of the original bridge, which had a central swing span of almost 150ft. The largest narrow-gauge swing-bridge in Britain, this was destroyed on the outbreak of World War 2 to prevent its use by an invading army. *Author*

Left: Rusting track at Blackwater Quay, seen in June 1999. The barges and fishing-smacks have largely been replaced by pleasure craft. The harbour branch was opened in 1914 and was never used for passenger services, closing in 1929, after just 15 years of freight use. The track seen here has remained unused for over 60 years. *Author*

Below: The sole surviving item of rolling stock from the Southwold Railway was a covered four-wheeled luggage van, which was rescued from an allotment and displayed at Southwold station for a time. It is seen in this view, taken in September 1999, preserved at the East Anglia Transport Museum at Carlton Colville. *Author's collection*

5 Saturdays-only to Sand Hutton

The death of Sir Robert Walker, of Sand Hutton Hall, in 1930 was accompanied by the demise of the Sand Hutton Light Railway shortly after. This demonstrates the link that existed between some narrow-gauge lines and their enthusiastic owners. The Sand Hutton was one of an interesting array of narrow-gauge lines that could once be found operating in the grounds of great country estates. Not just the toys of their owners, these lines provided useful freight links, particularly for coal and provisions, to the great houses. The locomotives used on the early lines were often functional, rather than fine miniature scale models.

The history of such lines extends back to 1874, when Sir Arthur Heywood built a 3¾-mile-long 15in-gauge line in the grounds of Duffield Bank, near Derby; the system was to close on his death in 1916. By 1895 Eaton Hall, near Chester, could boast of a 3-mile line linking the estate with the GWR's Balderton station; this system ran until 1946. The Blakesley Hall Railway, near Towcester, was opened in 1901, and linked the estate with nearby Blakesley station on the Stratford-on-Avon & Midland Junction Railway. The estate railway closed in 1939 and Blakesley Hall itself was demolished in 1957.

The most extensive and best-known system was the Sand Hutton Light Railway that ran in the Derwent Valley, to the east of York. The railway was first established in 1910, as a 15in-gauge private miniature railway, in the grounds of Sand Hutton Hall.

In 1920 a Light Railway Order was obtained, with the purpose of upgrading and extending the railway for passenger traffic. Four locomotives were eventually obtained, together with surplus material from the WD Deptford Meat Depot in London. In 1921-2 the existing line was converted to 1ft 6in gauge. The line was also extended to connect with the North Eastern Railway station at Warthill, on the York to Hull main line. By April 1922 a 1½-mile line was built to the Claxton brickworks and a line was also extended to Kissthorns. The following year the growing network was expanded to Bossall and Barnby House, this latter terminus being some 5¼ miles from Warthill. An extension across the River Derwent to Scrayingham was also authorised, but

Right: Sir Robert Walker drives *Synolda*, on his 15in-gauge Sand Hutton Railway. The locomotive was built by Bassett-Lowke, at Northampton in 1912, for the Sand Hutton estate. On the re-gauging of the line in 1922 to 18in, the locomotive was transferred to a pleasure line at Southend-on-Sea, before ending up at Manchester's Belle Vue Zoo. Upon closure of the zoo in 1968, it was rescued and restored for occasional use on the Ravenglass & Eskdale Railway. *Locomotive Publishing Co*

never built, the cost of the river bridge proving to be prohibitive.

The extensive system that developed was used for both agricultural produce and for the conveyance of bricks. At Warthill, freight could be transferred directly into standard-gauge trucks. Two narrow-gauge lines flanked the standard-gauge siding; that on the level allowed goods to be offloaded onto the Sand Hutton system, while a raised siding and mobile hoist allowed outgoing freight to be lowered into standard-gauge wagons. Some 75 2-ton ex-WD wagons made up the substantial goods stock, and indeed the Claxton brickworks at one time produced 20,000 bricks a day, requiring up to three locomotives to be in steam on the system.

The line also conveyed passengers, and several halts were provided. Passengers were carried in a single 30-seat coach that operated with a mobile buffet. However, there was a limited service of just three trains in each direction, on Saturdays only, between Warthill and Bossall. The passenger service ran from October 1924 until July 1930, and a Wednesday service was also provided in 1925.

The centre of the system was at Sand Hutton, where the engine shed was located. The Hall itself was served by the grandiosely-titled Sand Hutton Central. The station was in fact little more than a halt with a gravel platform and wooden hut!

Sir Robert died in 1930. Although it appears that passengers were still using trains the following year, the system had been making losses since the closure of Claxton brickworks in 1929, and it was therefore decided to close all the lines at the end of June 1932. This was a time of economic depression, and sadly the last work for some of the railway staff was to cut up the attractive Hunslet locomotives on-site.

Today, Sand Hutton Hall has been demolished and little remains of the railway. However, the route between Claxton brickworks and Claxton is clearly visible, as are the remains of the brickworks and clay pits. Small traces of line can be found elsewhere. The carriage body survived as a pavilion at a cricket club and has since been rescued. In 1959 Warthill main-line station closed, being followed by the main line itself in 1965 (see *Lost Lines — North Eastern*).

Below left: A Sand Hutton passenger train runs through woods on the 18in-gauge Sand Hutton Light Railway. The locomotive is a Hunslet 0-4-0WT, originally built in 1917 for War Department use at the Deptford Meat Depot in London. Sir Robert Walker purchased the locomotive and named it *Esme*, after his wife, in 1921. *LPC*

Above: One of the 0-4-0WT locomotives, working on the Sand Hutton Light Railway, with a covered van and bogie saloon carriage. The carriage was the only one operated by the railway and was built in 1924. With 36 seats and a mobile buffet, it was quite a sizeable vehicle for such a small gauge. On the closure of the railway, the coach survived as a cricket pavilion, before being saved for preservation. *LPC*

Centre right: Hunslet 0-4-0WT retaining its original Deptford No 12 plate. It is seen here hauling a van and the Sand Hutton Railway's coach on one of the Saturdays-only passenger services which ran for a short period between 1924 and 1930. *LPC*

Right: No 12 with its former Deptford number, after arrival on the Sand Hutton system. The second-hand Hunslet-built engines used on the line dated from 1915-17 and were particularly attractive. Sadly all four were all cut up on-site after the Sand Hutton Light Railway's closure in 1932. *LPC*

Left: Not much remains of the railway or Sand Hutton Hall, which has been demolished, but a clear indication of where the track once ran, near the former Claxton brickworks, is seen here in September 1999. *Author's collection*

Centre left: Claxton brickworks at one time produced 20,000 bricks a day. Remains of the railway, including some rotting sleepers, are still to be found within the trees that have reclaimed the works area since its closure in 1929. The clay-pits have become flooded and the tranquil area today is a far cry from the activity that was once to be found here, as can be seen in this view, taken in September 1999. *Author's collection*

Below left: Although all the delightful Leeds-built Hunslet 0-4-0WTs that operated the Sand Hutton system were scrapped, an engine of similar design and gauge, from the John Knowles clay works in Leicestershire, was preserved. *Jack*, a Hunslet dating from 1898, can be seen in this view, taken in 1990, at the Leeds Industrial Museum. *T. Heavyside*

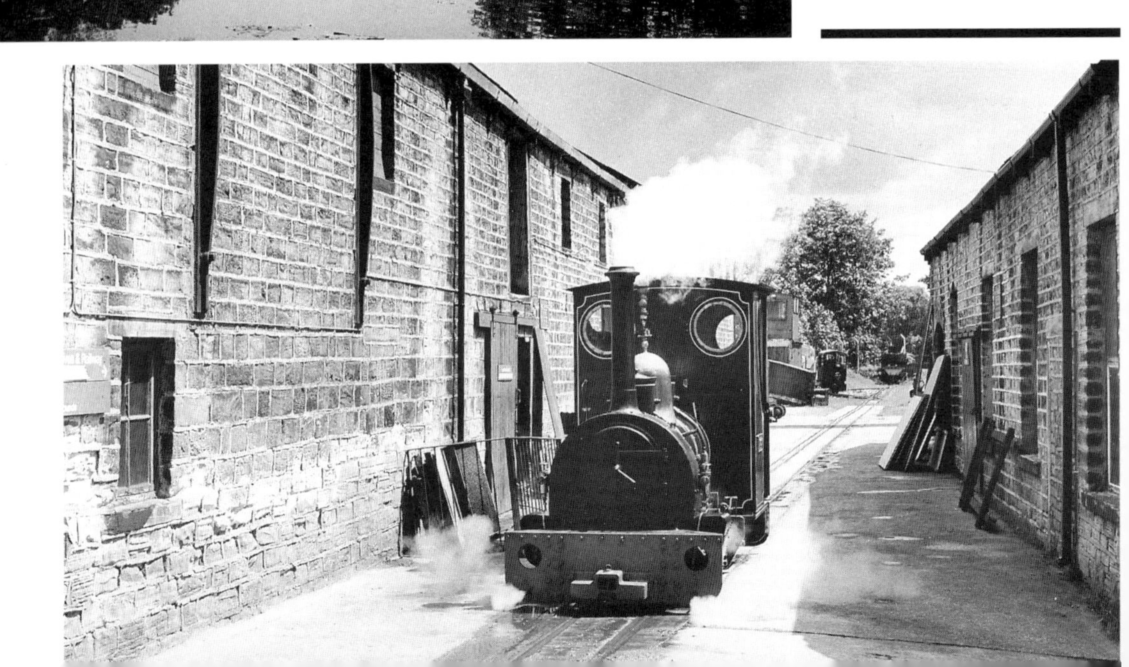

6 The Clyde to Campbeltown

Clyde steamers sailing to Campbeltown in the 1932 summer season were no longer greeted by the welcoming whistle of the Campbeltown & Machrihanish Light Railway. The remote and rugged Scottish Highlands appear well suited for the construction of narrow-gauge railways. Indeed, at one time there were schemes for over 150 miles of narrow-gauge railway in the north of Scotland, including a line from Garve to Ullapool. As it turned out, few narrow-gauge passenger lines were built in Scotland.

Several Scottish collieries operated narrow-gauge lines, and it was coal on the Kintyre peninsula that led to the opening of Scotland's only narrow-gauge public passenger railway (other than Glasgow's underground). A 3-mile coal canal was opened in 1794 to serve the collieries in the area, but a colliery railway opened from Campbeltown in 1877 and was extended to new pits at Drumlemble in 1881.

By the summer of 1906 passengers were carried, once the original 2ft 3in-gauge route had been upgraded and extended under the provisions of the Light Railway Act. The new 6-mile route ran right across Kintyre, from the Atlantic coast at Machrihanish to Hall Street and the quayside at Campbeltown. In 1906 and 1907 new locomotives *Argyll* and *Atlantic* were introduced on the line, supplementing the two remaining smaller colliery engines. The new 0-6-2T locomotives were attractive and powerful, whilst the six new passenger coaches were particularly elegant and were generally regarded as some of the finest ever built for a narrow-gauge railway.

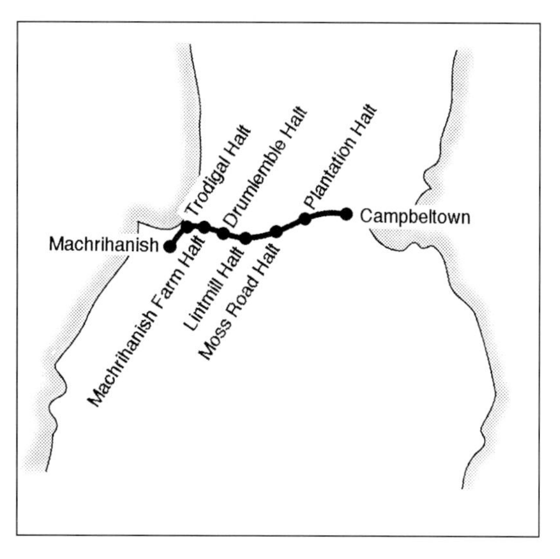

In 1907 consideration was given to further extensions of the line. However, plans to build along the rocky eastern coast of Kintyre towards Tayinloan and south to Southend were regretfully — but probably quite rightly — never implemented.

Although there was a limited passenger service, in 1910 a 5.50am departure from Campbeltown provided an early-morning train for workers in the

Right: Waverley, the world's last sea-going paddle-steamer, was also the last 'paddler' built for the LNER. The frequency of Clyde steamer services to Campbeltown gradually reduced, and by 1974 all services had ended. This view, taken in September 1999, was a special excursion by *Waverley* 'doon the watter' to Campbeltown. *Author*

area. Six intermediate halts were made available on the line, notwithstanding that these were simply road crossing points, with no facilities provided. Clyde steamers arriving at Campbeltown also added useful passenger traffic, and the railway was eager to make it known to intending passengers that the Clyde steamers would not depart until the railway passengers had returned to Campbeltown. A trip on the line to Machrihanish, where facilities included a golf course, on occasions enabled the calm of Campbeltown Loch to be contrasted with the wrath of the Atlantic coast.

The transportation of coal, from pits near Machrihanish to the port at Campbeltown, continued to be the main purpose of the line. Over 150 wagons, some in private ownership, were at one time provided for this service. The coal was loaded onto colliers at Campbeltown by a 4-ton crane. From 1926, however, coal traffic declined, and by 1929 the Argyll colliery had hit a geological fault and was forced to close.

Financial problems for the railway mounted, and by 1931 buses had replaced trains outside the summer peak. Despite the quality of the carriages, bus competition increased the line's difficulties. Passenger trains ceased in September 1931, after just 25 years of service. In May of the following year an attempt to restore services was thwarted by the need for locomotive repairs, and the railway closed to all traffic soon after. By 1934 the line had been dismantled. The locomotives were scrapped and for a time some of the coaches were used as accommodation in a local boatyard and elsewhere in the area. Today, little remains, but the station area at Machrihanish can still be identified, as can the deep cutting into Hall Street at Campbeltown, the former railway line being used here as a footpath.

In 1974 the regular BR steamer services 'doon the watter' to Campbeltown were withdrawn, although the *Waverley* — the sole surviving Clyde paddle-steamer — still provides the occasional excursion to Campbeltown.

The Royal Mail Route to CAMPBELTOWN & MACHRIHANISH Per "DAVAAR" or "KINLOCH."

Via LOCHRANZA and CARRADALE.—Leaving **Glasgow** Central Station, to **Gourock** daily 8 25 a.m. and from **Glasgow**, St. Enoch Station, to **Princes Pier** daily 7 55 a.m.; returning from **Campbeltown** daily 8 a.m.

For full particulars, see Glasgow newspapers. Telegrams, "Davaar, Campbeltown." R. M. Dunlop, 8, Kingston Dock, Glasgow; P. McCallum, Custom House Quay, Greenock, Agents.

[J.R.] **ROSS WALLACE, Manager, Campbeltown.**

Campbeltown 1924.
Crown copyright

Above: Chevalier, a 0-4-2ST built by Andrew Barclay and one of the original colliery engines taken over by the Campbeltown & Machrihanish Light Railway. It is seen here outside Limecraigs shed at Campbeltown, on 12 May 1925. The locomotive was withdrawn in 1931. *Ian Allan Library*

Below: The extension of the line down into Hall Street at Campbeltown made connection with Clyde steamers, at the end of the quay, particularly convenient. There were no raised platforms at any of the stations, and at Campbeltown the train simply waited in the middle of the street. *Bucknall Collection*

GYLL
PHIC STUDIO

ROYAL HOTEL

Left: Atlantic, one of the two 0-6-2T Barclay locomotives built for the railway. It is seen here in Hall Street at Campbeltown on 2 August 1930. In May 1932 it was decided to cease using the line; the locomotive was transferred to T. Ward of Sheffield, but had been scrapped by 1934. *H. C. Casserley*

Below left: Smaller steamships could berth in the inner dock at Campbeltown, allowing a short walk to the train. This view of Hall Street shows a four-coach train, headed by *Atlantic*, waiting to depart on 2 August 1930. *H. C. Casserley*

Above right: All six of the attractive Pickering-built bogie saloons, with their end balconies and distinctive curved white roofs, are seen here. These coaches were generally recognised as some of the best ever built for any British narrow-gauge railway. The double-headed train is seen *en route* to Machrihanish. *SLS*

Right: 0-6-2T *Argyll* is seen waiting to depart from Machrihanish station. The Atlantic Ocean is to be found below the distant crofts. The breeze is clearly blowing towards the fence in the foreground serving as a makeshift clothes-line. Let's hope the engine does not create too much sooty smoke on departure! *Ian Allan Library*

Below: Machrihanish 1924. *Crown copyright*

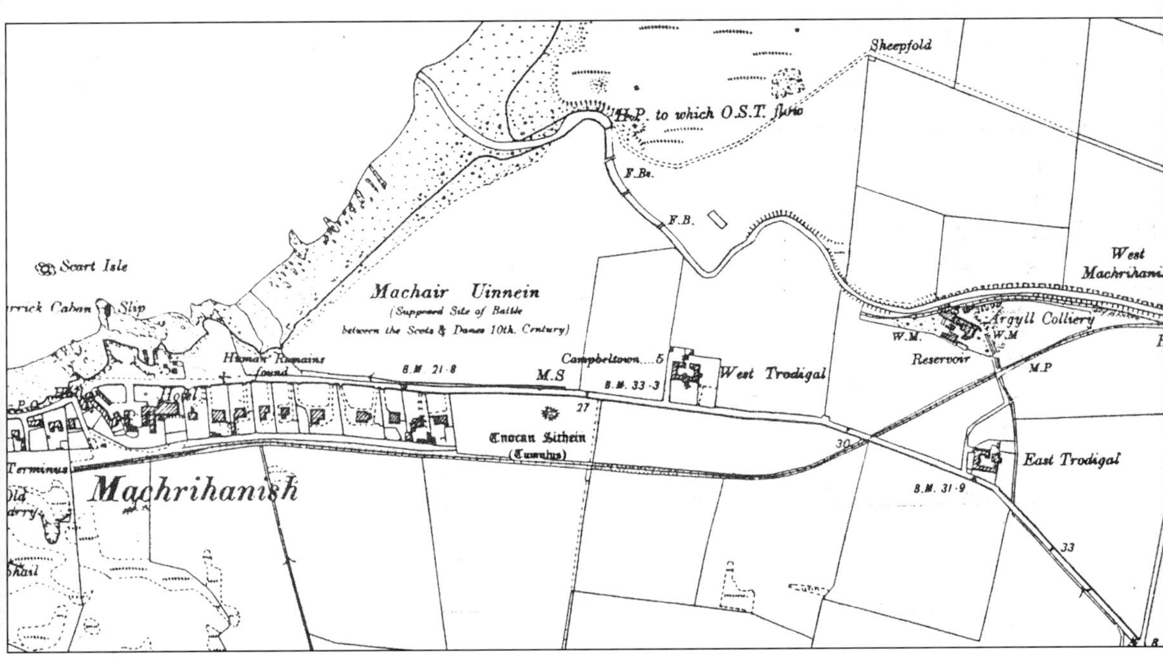

Above: Argyll and a four-coach train wait to depart from Machrihanish, where an attractive (but small) station building was provided. Although additional housing has been built in the area since this view was taken, the route of the line leading to the station is still discernible. *Ian Allan Library*

Below: Hall Street at Campbeltown, seen here in September 1999. Cars have replaced the trains, but much remains the same today as when the railway operated. A working scale model of the quayside section of the railway is to be found at the Campbeltown Heritage Centre. *Author*

Below right: A view of the extended line, down into Hall Street at Campbeltown, in September 1999. The extension involved a deep cutting, and the spoil from this was used to create The Strand, a recreational lawn area reclaimed from Campbeltown Loch. The 1 in 35 curved gradient of the extended line from the quayside at Hall Street provided a strenuous climb for the railway's locomotives. *Author*

7 The mysterious Manifold

In March 1934 just seven passengers travelled on the last train on the Leek & Manifold Valley Light Railway. The line was built under the provisions of the Light Railway Act of 1896 and was seen as an opportunity to open up an isolated and beautiful part of the Peak District. The 2ft 6in-gauge, 8¾-mile line opened in June 1904. It connected with the standard-gauge North Staffordshire Railway at the interchange station of Waterhouses. From its opening the line was worked and maintained by the North Staffordshire Railway.

The railway climbed on a steady gradient up the Manifold Valley, towards Hulme End. It included a 154yd tunnel and numerous river bridges over the mysterious River Manifold, which disappears into the Peak District's 'underground' system for part of its course, leaving a dry riverbed on the surface for much of the year.

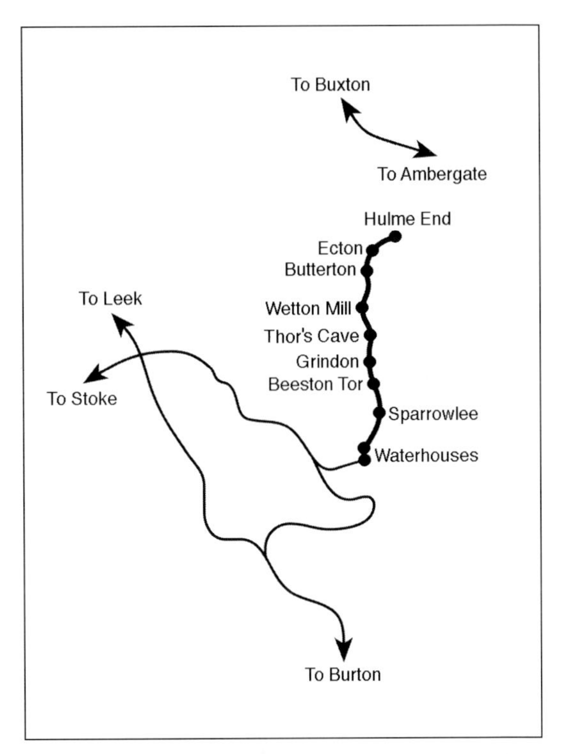

Below: A Leek & Manifold train, showing a standard-gauge wagon on one of the narrow-gauge transporter trucks. The railway was the first in England to make use of such trucks, enabling standard-gauge wagons to travel over the narrow gauge while avoiding the trans-shipment of freight. *SLS*

There are other apparent mysteries associated with the railway, and the building of the line to a narrow gauge is perhaps one of these. It was a substantially-constructed railway, built to the highest standards under the direction of Everard Calthrop, with curves and grades largely acceptable for standard gauge. Furthermore, as originally planned, the aim was to link with two existing standard-gauge lines.

The line showed off the Peak District at its very best; the white limestone rock-faces and deep-sided gorges are most attractive, and intermediate stations with names such as Sparrowlee, Beeston Tor and Thor's Cave may well have encouraged tourism. The line's four coaches were also designed with large windows and observation balconies to view the scenery. Yet a further mystery surrounds the approach to tourist traffic. The sightseeing potential of the line was clearly evident, but the railway never really developed this side of its operations. The milk traffic required a seven-day service, but for the most part a sparse passenger service was provided. When the nearby Potteries had their annual holiday and excursion traffic was heavy, the passenger stock was simply inadequate, although, to be fair, cleaned-up goods wagons and all available items of rolling stock were pressed into passenger service.

In other respects the narrow-gauge line was a pioneer in reducing interchange problems, having four transporter wagons. The narrow-gauge sidings at Waterhouses were at a lower level than the standard-gauge track, thus enabling standard-gauge wagons — more often than not milk tanks — to be low-loaded directly onto the narrow-gauge transporter wagons. Similarly, at several stations a short length of standard-gauge track was provided for standard-gauge wagons.

The railway's two locomotives, *E. R. Calthrop* and *J. B. Earle*, were particularly distinctive, being basically scaled-down versions of those for the Barsi Light Railway in India. The 2-6-4Ts were designed to run on lightweight track and each operated complete with a huge headlight, giving a colonial appearance.

The original plan had been for the line to connect with Longnor and the LNWR line to Buxton. Had this been achieved, Hulme End would have been the halfway point, and consequently the locomotive shed and main depot was located here. Yet, as built, the line basically ran from one isolated locality to another, and financial losses mounted after World War 1. The numerous stations were also poorly sited for the hamlets they served, and were unable to compete with local bus services.

In 1923 the railway became the only narrow-gauge passenger line outside Ireland to form part of the LMS, and the locomotives, which originally sported a chocolate livery, were repainted in Midland red. However, the promise of Buxton had never materialised, Ecton creamery closed and the milk traffic was lost. There were mounting losses, and the LMS inevitably announced the closure of the route. The last trains ran in March 1934.

After closure, in a pioneering scheme to provide recreational facilities, the railway was handed over by the LMS to Staffordshire County Council. The line was dismantled and converted into a footpath, while in 1953 the section between Redhurst and Butterton became a single-track road. Consequently, the entire route is still extant, along with station buildings at Waterhouses and Hulme End, all the bridges and Swainsley Tunnel.

Below left: Close-up of the Kitson-built 2-6-4T No 1 *E. R. Calthrop*, named after the engineer responsible for the design and construction of the line. The engine is seen here taking water at Hulme End, the main depot on the line. The locomotive was scrapped in 1937 after closure of the railway. *Bucknall Collection*

Above: No 2 *J. B. Earle*, an identical locomotive to No 1, at Hulme End with the two-coach 3.45pm train to Waterhouses, on 29 April 1933. The station name-board announced that Hulme End was also the station 'for Sheen and Hartington', two equally-tiny nearby settlements. *Ian Allan Library*

Below: No 1 *E. R. Calthrop* eases two standard-gauge milk tanks, on the 2ft 6in-gauge transporter trucks, out of Ecton creamery, prior to its closure in 1932. The creamery building, next to the railway in the background, contained hundreds of the old-style milk churns. The spoil in the far background was from a former copper mine. *Bucknall Collection*

MANIFOLD
VALLEY
VISITOR
CENTRE
PUBLIC
TOILETS

Left: Hulme End passenger station and the remains of the shed, to the right, seen here in June 1999. The old station booking hall is now a visitor centre and museum. Hulme End itself remains a small hamlet. *Author*

Below far left: The 154yd Swainsley Tunnel, near Butterton. The tunnel was constructed to conceal the railway from Swainsley Hall, rather than to overcome any physical obstructions in the valley. It is seen here in June 1999, illuminated for its current cycle and road use. *Author*

Bottom left: The north portal of Swainsley Tunnel, in June 1999. Both stone tunnel portals were of similar designs. The brick-lined tunnel was the major engineering work on the line. During World War 2 the tunnel was used as a munitions store and the entrances were sealed. *Author*

Above right: One of the bridges over the dry River Manifold is viewed here, near Wetton Mill, in June 1999. The river follows an underground course during drier periods, but springs into life during the winter, or at particularly wet periods. *Author*

Centre right: The substantially-built stone subway steps to Waterhouses interchange station, seen here in derelict condition in December 1958. *Hugh Davies*

Below right: The remaining wooden station buildings at the interchange station at Waterhouses, in June 1999. The narrow-gauge trains used the north side of the station where the platform was a mere 6in high. The building currently acts as a bike-hire depot; it is possible to cycle the entire length of the former narrow-gauge line, to Hulme End. *Author*

8 Glimpses of the Glyn Valley

July 1935 saw the remaining freight services on the Glyn Valley Tramway slip quietly away. The line ran beside the roadway for much of its length along the Glyn Valley, and was always fondly known as 'the tram', although in many respects it was more of a railway than a tramway in character.

The first line to open along the Glyn Valley, in 1873, was a horse- and gravity-worked tramway. The 2ft 4¼ in-gauge line, exactly half standard gauge, ran between Glyn Ceiriog and Pontfaen and then over a heavily-graded section to the Shropshire Union Canal at Rhoswiel. Passengers were carried between 1874 and 1886, but freight was rapidly increasing from quarries in the area and it was decided to upgrade the line.

The Tramway Acts allowed steam engines to be used on roadside lines, and between 1886 and 1888 the line was reconstructed as a locomotive-operated tramway; the new passenger line ran between Glyn Ceiriog, Pontfaen and Chirk. Curiously, on reopening, ¼ in was added to the gauge, possibly as a result of the track being spread by contractors' locomotives from the nearby Snailbeach District Railways. Chirk was located on both the GWR Ruabon to Oswestry main line and the Llangollen arm of the Shropshire Union Canal. However, a number of local difficulties meant

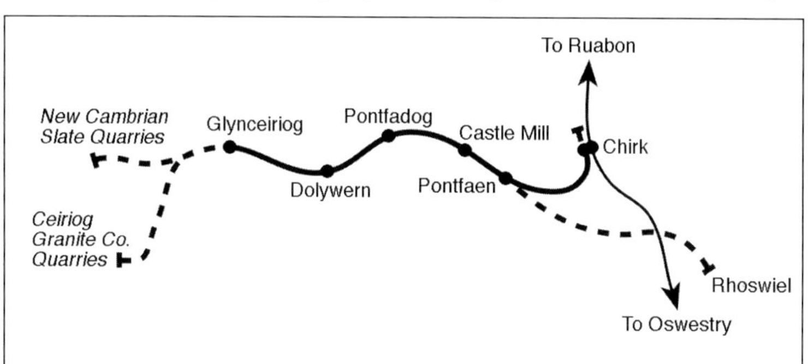

Below right: The Chirk area in 1914. *Crown copyright*

Below: No 1 *Dennis*, seen here at Chirk on 30 May 1932. This 0-4-2T Beyer Peacock tram engine was built at Gorton Foundry in Manchester in 1888. It was scrapped, along with all the other locomotives, after the closure of the line in 1936. *H. C. Casserley*

Above: No 2 *Sir Theodore*, a Beyer Peacock 0-4-2T tram engine, was also built in Manchester in 1888. The locomotive is seen here with a mixed train of five coaches and two wagons at Chirk station. The faded initials of the Glyn Valley Tramway can just be discerned on the locomotive, while just visible in the distance is Chirk GWR main-line signalbox. *Ian Allan Library*

Left: The ornate crest of the Glyn Valley Tramway, seen here on one of the surviving coaches on the Talyllyn Railway. *Author*

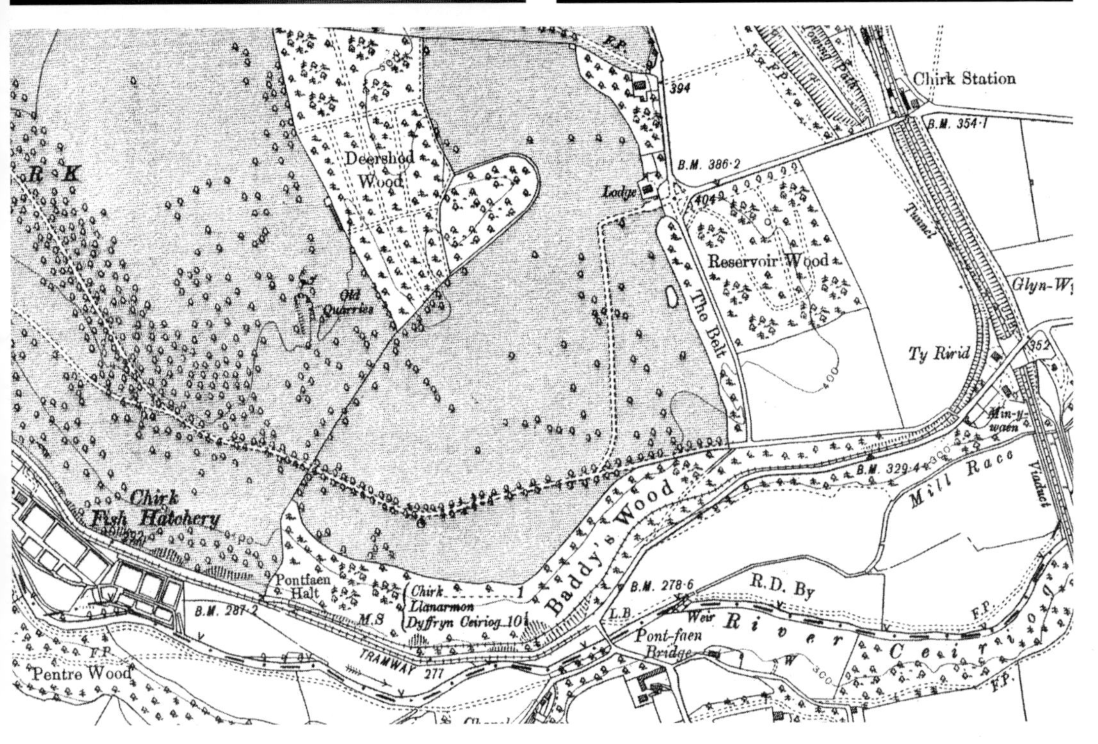

that a line to wharves on the canal basin and a passenger interchange with the GWR's Chirk station were not opened until 1891.

Freight-only lines were also extended up the valley beyond Glyn Ceiriog to quarries in the area. The woollen mills at Glyn Ceiriog contributed some goods traffic, but slate and granite roadstone were the main freight to use the line. At its peak, over 200 wagons were provided, and after World War 1 an ex-WD Baldwin was added to the existing stock of three locomotives.

Despite the investment, the independent and isolated line was not able to compete with road transport. On the passenger side, some tourists were carried, but weekday-only trains of antiquated stock took up to 40 minutes to cover the 6½-mile passenger section. Buses linked directly with Oswestry, and the line closed to passengers in April 1933

On the freight side, from 1926 a new access road allowed lorries direct entry to one of the main quarries served by the tramway. For a time the tramway managed to get lorries to load granite onto its wagons, but this could not save the line; the locomotives were in a declining state of repair, and the tramway closed to all traffic in July 1935.

The line was dismantled in 1936, and much track was sold to the nearby Gresford Colliery for use in new workings; the locomotives had been cut up at Chirk by 1937. However, some of the mineral sidings on the upper part of the line continued in use until the closure of the remaining quarries in the early 1950s.

Considerable sections of the old line can still be traced; indeed, part of the route beyond Glyn Ceiriog is a National Trust footpath. Two coaches exist on the Talyllyn Railway, while the Glyn Valley Tramway Group has restored the waiting room at Pontfadog, which acts as a small museum. The locomotive shed at Glyn Ceiriog is to become a tramway heritage centre, and the long-term objective is to reopen the line.

CHIRK, PONTFADOG, and GLYNCEIRIOG.—Glyn Valley.
Sec. and Man., G. M. Jenkins.

Miles	Up.	Week Days. mrn	aft	aft Except Weds.	aft Weds.	aft					
	Chirk ....dep.	9 50	1 35	3 20	4 10	6K30	....	....	....	....	....
1¼	Pontfaen	Sig.	Sig.	Sig.	Sig.	Sig.	....	....	....	....	....
2	Castle Mill..........	10 1	1 46	3 30	4 21	6 39	....	....	....	....	....
4	Pontfadog..........	1013	1 58	3 40	4 33	6 49	....	....	....	....	....
5	Dolywern	1021	2 6	3 48	4 41	6 56	....	....	....	....	....
6½	Glynceiriog....arr.	1030	2 15	3 55	4 50	7 5	....	....	....	....	....

Miles	Down.	Week Days. mrn	mrn Weds.	aft	aft Sats.	aft Except Weds.	aft Weds.	aft Weds.	aft	
	Glynceiriog......dep.	8 5	1120	1225	2 30	4 0	4 15	5 5	7 20	....
1½	Dolywern	8 14	1129	1234	2 39	4 9	4 24	5 14	7 29	....
2½	Pontfadog..........	8 22	1137	1242	2 46	4 17	4 32	5 21	7 37	....
4½	Castle Mill..........	8 34	1149	1254	2 56	4 26	4 41	5 31	7 48	....
5¼	Pontfaen	Sig.	Sig.	Sig.	Sig.	Sig.	Sig.	Sig.	Sig.	....
6½	Chirk 75, 80 .....arr.	8 45	12 0	1 5	3 5	4 35	4 50	5 40	8 2	....

K Waits for the 2 15 aft. from Paddington for Passengers for the Glyn Valley Line, on notice being given beforehand.

Left: Passenger services provided on the line in 1910.

Below left: No 2 *Sir Theodore* is seen here at Glyn Ceiriog on 28 August 1926. The locomotive heads a 12-coach excursion train, which includes of all but three of the tramway's four-wheeled coaching stock. *Bucknall Collection*

Right: No 3 *Glyn* poses for the camera with some of its tramway wheel-skirts raised, in about 1910. The livery at this time was unlined green. The engine was scrapped in 1936, but a nameplate survives at the narrow-gauge museum at Tywyn. *LPC*

Centre right: 'The Baldwin', as it was always known, ran on the line without tramway-style skirts. The American firm of Baldwin built the 4-6-0T locomotive in 1917 for military use. It was re-gauged and provided with a modified chimney by Beyer Peacock before delivery to the tramway in 1921. The livery in this view was black with white lining. The locomotive was scrapped in 1936. *Ian Allan Library*

Below: No 3 *Glyn*, a Beyer Peacock 0-4-2T tram engine built in 1892, is seen here with passenger stock near Chirk. The engine was scrapped after the closure of the line in 1936. *Bucknall Collection*

Left: Pontfadoc station has been preserved by the Glyn Valley Tramway Group and is seen here in June 1999. The former waiting room boasted seats and an open fire, but such luxury was still unable to compete with the motorbus. *Author*

Centre left: Some remains of the tramway are to be found at Chirk, including a bridge near the former GWR main-line station. This was one of the few bridges over the Glyn Valley Tramway. The view seen here was taken in July 1999. *Author's collection*

Below left: Two coach bodies survived in the Glyn Valley area after closure of the tramway. Originally built by the Midland Railway Carriage & Wagon Co, one of the two beautifully-preserved Glyn Valley coaches, in green and cream livery, is seen here at Tywyn on the Talyllyn Railway, in June 1999. *Author*

Right: Exe receives attention to its motion on a down train to Blackmoor Gate. One of the three original 2-6-2T Manning Wardle engines built for the line, it is pictured here in the medium green Lynton & Barnstaple livery, in pre-Southern Railway days. Covered van No 6 is seen immediately behind the locomotive. *Bucknall Collection*

9 A legend to Lynton

In September 1935, a matter of weeks after the closure of the Glyn Valley line and in contrast to the Leek & Manifold, over 300 passengers travelled on the last train on the Lynton & Barnstaple Railway. There was genuine sadness at the closure of this railway, and over a thousand people waited in the rain at Barnstaple station to witness the arrival of the last train.

Promoted by local interests, the Lynton & Barnstaple was a heavily-engineered railway and, at 19½ miles, the longest and arguably finest of all the English narrow-gauge lines. Opened in May 1898, the picturesque 1ft 11½in-gauge railway ran from the interchange station with the LSWR at Barnstaple Town, before snaking its way through the wooded valley of the River Yeo and passing over the shoulder of Exmoor to reach the north Devon coast. The line was steeply graded, and climbed for 8 miles at 1 in 50 to reach a summit of almost 1,000ft near Woody Bay, before descending to the terminus at Lynton.

Building the line proved about twice as costly as anticipated, and involved the construction of the 133yd curving Chelfham Viaduct — the largest viaduct on any narrow-gauge passenger line in England. Deep cuttings, high embankments and distinctive cottage-style stations also characterised the route.

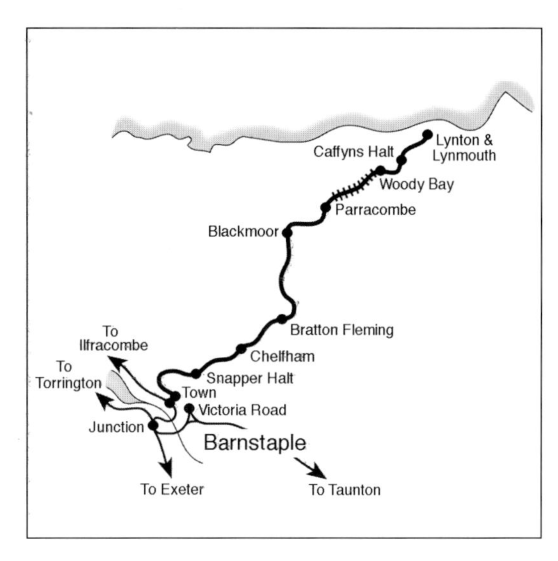

On opening, the new stock was equally distinguished. The wagons used a form of roller bearing and were vacuum-braked, enabling them to be used in mixed passenger trains. The three Manning Wardle locomotives, *Yeo*, *Exe* and *Taw*, were the heaviest 1ft 11½in-gauge conventional locomotives to

operate on such a narrow gauge in England. An American Baldwin called *Lyn* was rapidly added to the stock after the line opened, to cope with the traffic.

The Lynton & Barnstaple was absorbed by the Southern Railway in 1923. An effort was made to improve services, including the purchase of a further engine called *Lew*, of similar design to the original locomotives. Considerable funds were also spent on publicity. However, even though a nearby cliff lift was provided, the elevated position of the station at Lynton was not entirely convenient for the beautiful resort of Lynmouth located below. The cost of new rails and the wages of nearly 60 staff, combined with mounting winter losses, led the Southern Railway to close the line in September 1935.

The Reverend Chanter of Parracombe had scattered flower seeds from the windows of the trains, and the line was held in great local affection. To the shriek of whistles and explosion of detonators, the last train came to a stand at Barnstaple and the Lynton & Barnstaple line was dead — or was it? A wreath was seen to bear the inscription 'Perchance it is not dead but sleepeth'. These words have come to haunt those who can see the great potential of this line; had the railway survived only a few more years it would today be one of Britain's greatest railway attractions.

After closure, little time was wasted in lifting the track and scrapping the stock. However, much of the route and its physical infrastructure remain. *Lew*, just over a decade old, was shipped to Brazil, where it seemingly vanished without trace, while coach bodies survive, including one on the Ffestiniog Railway and one at the NRM. The aim of the Lynton & Barnstaple Society is to reopen the line. Already Chelfham, Woody Bay and Parracombe stations, together with a stretch of the old route, have been acquired, and a rebuild of one of the attractively-proportioned Manning Wardle locomotives has been undertaken. In the long term, the legendary Lynton & Barnstaple may well have every prospect of losing its 'lost line' status.

Below: Yeo, No 759 (as numbered by the Southern Railway), waits to depart from Lynton & Lynmouth station with a three-coach train, in Southern days. The leading carriage is one of the popular observation saloons used on the line. Electric lighting had been installed on the station platform as part of a package of improvements provided by the Southern Railway when this view was taken, in September 1935. *Ian Allan Library*

Below right: Alternative ways of reaching Lynton and Lynmouth, from the 1930 *Red Rail Guide*.

Right: Taw, No 761, with a Sunday special, is given the right of way at Blackmoor in May 1935. The well-kept engine and coaches are to be noted, while the attractiveness of the line was originally enhanced by a £5 prize, which was awarded annually by Sir George Newnes to the station with the best-kept flower-beds.
Ian Allan Library

Centre right: The charming switchback nature of this much-lamented line is apparent from this view of a train hauled by *Yeo* leaving Chelfham Viaduct, which looks to be almost at right-angles to the train.
Ian Allan Library

Below right: Lyn, the American Baldwin — No 762 in Southern Railway days — is seen here at Barnstaple. Soon after the line's opening, it was discovered that additional motive power was required urgently, and *Lyn* arrived in crates from America in 1899. The locomotive was a success on the line, particularly because of its enhanced water-storage capacity.
Ian Allan Library

LYNTON & LYNMOUTH (Devon). **231¼** miles. From **Waterloo. Fares, 43/4a, 26/0c;** Return, **86/8a,** 52/0c. Week-end, 57/9a, 34/9c. Pop. (Lynton) 2,587.

W'loo.	Lynton	Lynton	W'loo.
AM11 0r	5 57	AM7 13r	2 8
—	—	9 25r	4 0
—	—	PM1242r	8 38
—	—	3 36‡	4 0f
—	—	—	—
—	—	—	—
—	—	—	—

No Sunday Service.

f—a.m.
r—Restaurant Car.
‡—Mons., Weds. & Sats. only.

Another Route. From Paddington, via Taunton and Barnstaple. 209 miles. Same fares.

Pad.	Lynton	Lynton	Pad.
AM1 40k	1148	AM7 13r	4 5
5 30k	3 8	PM1242r	9 0
1030‡	5 57	3 36k	2 40f
—	—	—	—
—	—	—	—

No Sunday Service.

f—a.m.
r—Restaurant Car.
k—Mons., Weds. & Sats. only.
‡—By Taunton Slip Carriage.

Another route. From Paddington, via Minehead and Road Motor thence (week-days only). Fares, 43/6 a, 39/6c; Return, 86/0a, 57/0c Week-end, 56/9a, 38/0c.

Pad.	Lynton	Lynton	Pad.
AM1030‡	4 15	AM9 20r	4 5
—	—	—	—
—	—	—	—
—	—	—	—

f—a.m.
r—Restaurant Car.
‡—By Slip Carriage.

Above: Manning Wardle 2-6-2Ts No 759 *Yeo* and No 761 *Taw*, both dating from 1898, double-head a train at Pilton in 1935, during the last summer of services. *A. MacLeod*

Left: Barnstaple and Pilton areas in 1920. *Crown copyright*

Right: This view could well be of a shed in America, but *Lyn* is seen here in deepest Devon, at Pilton shed. The locomotive was still in service up until closure of the line in 1935, but was sold for scrap for £50. *Ian Allan Library*

Centre right: Exe and *Taw* being maintained and having their boilers washed out in the two-road Pilton shed at Barnstaple, on 17 June 1926. Note the square front buffers. Both engines were scrapped in 1935, but the shed remained until destroyed by a fire in 1992. *H. C. Casserley*

Below: Caffyns Halt, between Woody Bay and Lynton. The halt was a later addition to the line and opened to serve the nearby golf course in 1907. After closure it became a farm store area. The bridge remains, but the site of the request halt has since been cleared. *J. Palm*

Above: The former station at Woody Bay, long after closure. This was once one of the more important intermediate stations on the line, but plans to develop the resort and provide a coastal steamer service never materialised. The Lynton & Barnstaple Railway Society purchased the station in 1995; if aims to reopen the line are achieved, trains will once again call at this station. *David Lawrence*

Below left: Lew in a remote coffee-plantation shed, after transshipment to Brazil? Actually this view is of a half-size replica of *Yeo* which is to be found on the Fairbourne Railway in Wales and it is seen here in June 1999. A further full-size locomotive, *Lyd*, has been built at Boston Lodge on the Ffestiniog Railway, and uses the chimney of the original *Yeo*. *Author*

Below right: Chelfham Viaduct was the largest viaduct on any narrow-gauge line in England. The eight curved yellow-brick arches extend for some 133yd and are up to 70ft high. This view was taken in 1995. The viaduct remains and, with appropriate remedial work, is in a condition suitable for reuse. *Author*

10 Fire over Jersey

In 1936 fire resulted in the premature closure of Jersey's narrow-gauge railway.

A line from St Helier to St Aubin was originally opened as a standard-gauge railway in September 1870. Much of the route was built along the coast of St Aubin's Bay, and the Island States paid for considerable sections of the associated new sea defences required. However, by 1874 the railway-owned hotel at St Aubin was losing money, as was the railway, which was declared *en désastre* (bankrupt), but trains continued to run in the public interest.

A planned extension of the line (that would have improved its viability by serving quarries) from St Aubin to Pont Marquet involved crossing a rugged part of the island. This area was more suited to narrow-gauge construction, and the line was built to a 3ft 6in gauge. At first there were plans to add a third rail to the standard-gauge line, providing a mixed-gauge route to St Helier. However, after some haggling, the existing 3¾-mile standard-gauge railway was converted to narrow 3ft 6in gauge in 1883-4. The new narrow-gauge line was extended to La Moye granite quarries in 1894,

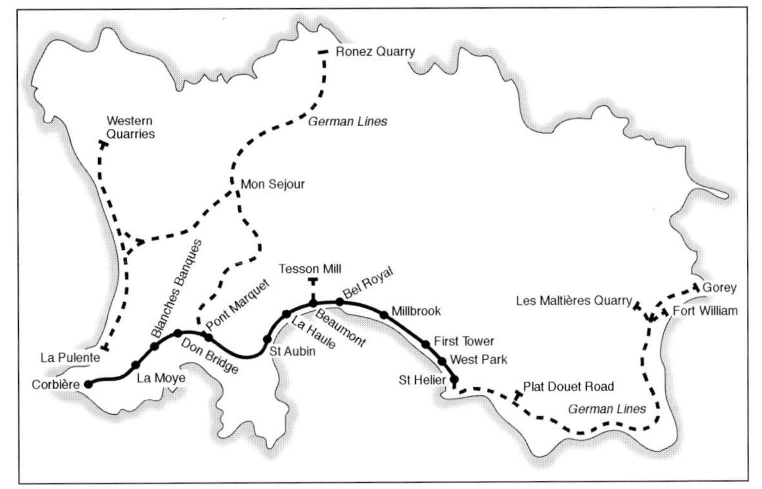

Below: Jersey Railways & Tramways' Bagnall-built 2-4-0T No 1 *St Heliers* at the Weighbridge terminus at St Helier c1900. The locomotive was scrapped following the decision not to reopen the railway for the 1937 season. *Ian Allan Library*

although it was not until the following year that the first passenger train ran from St Helier to La Moye.

In 1896 the line was taken over by the Jersey Railways & Tramways Ltd, and by June 1899 was extended further to a new terminus at Corbière, making a total length of line of 8½ miles. There was some granite freight, but summer tourists provided the main source of income, and in 1925 passenger numbers reached their peak, with over 1 million journeys being made. However, car numbers were increasing on the island, and the railway company also began to run buses. Economies were made, and in the winter of 1923 Sentinel steam railcars were introduced. In 1932 it was decided to withdraw the winter passenger services between St Aubin and Corbière, but there were no plans for closure.

Closure came prematurely and in an unforeseen way. During the winter the carriages were stored at St Aubin. In the early hours of 18 October 1936 a huge fire spread out of control, destroying 16 wooden carriages and badly damaging St Aubin station buildings and the Terminus Hotel. On viewing the wreckage it was decided that it would be impossible to reopen the line for the following summer season, and therefore the railway closed down.

Work on dismantling the railway was still proceeding when the German occupation of the Channel Islands began in July 1940. The Germans wished to fortify the island and rebuilt the line to metre-gauge. In addition, from Pont Marquet a new branch was built to the Ronez quarries. A new 1ft 11½in (60cm)-gauge line was also built along St Ouen's Bay, and even the standard-gauge line to Gorey was rebuilt to this gauge. Some 15 tank locomotives were requisitioned from France and Germany to work the lines, but an undertaking to consider passenger services never materialised. After the occupation ended, all the tracks were removed.

Today, the remains of the fine station buildings at St Helier and St Aubin, together with that at Corbière, can still be found. Considerable sections of the line have been converted into footpaths, and a narrow-gauge coach body that survived the fire remains on the island.

Below: An ex-German 0-6-0T from the Todt organisation, which was used on the island during World War 2. It is seen here at St Helier quayside, waiting to be scrapped, after hostilities had ended. It is of note that, beneath the single buffer, a second, double buffer-beam has been added, for use after the locomotive was requisitioned for wartime operation on Jersey. *Ian Allan Library*

Above: St Aubin station and the Terminus Hotel building survived the devastating fire to the coaching stock that ended the railway services. The building was in use as a police station when this view was taken in October 1998. Rather surprisingly, the clock was a later addition. *Author*

Right: St Helier station was rebuilt in 1901. Much of the imposing quayside terminal station remains in use as a tourist office, and a side view of the former station is seen here in October 1998. *Author*

Left: Many bridges and even a short tunnel are to be found on the rugged section of line from St Aubin to Corbière. The view seen here was taken on a rather wet day in October 1998. Much of this section of former line is now used as a long-distance footpath. *Author*

Centre left: Corbière station — a rather austere-looking building compared to those at St Helier and St Aubin, which are two of the most imposing of narrow-gauge stations. Trains from St Helier reached Corbière station in 35 minutes, and even romantic moonlight excursions were once run to this scenic terminus. *Author*

Below left: One of the original varnished-teak narrow-gauge Jersey Railways coaches that survived the great fire remains in a museum on the island. *Author's collection*

11 The South Snowdon phoenix

Many narrow-gauge railways regarded freight as their most important income, and some conveyed passengers in an almost indifferent fashion. Yet most narrow-gauge railway companies were equally entrepreneurial. North Wales is a lovely area and, as Victorian interest in mountains and the seaside grew, tourists to the area increased. The Snowdon Mountain Tramroad & Hotels Co Ltd, as it was known until 1928, developed entirely due to the scenic splendour of the area.

Another line to see the opportunity presented by tourists was the North Wales Narrow Gauge Railway. The 1ft 11½in-gauge line was opened in stages between 1877 and 1881, from Dinas to Rhyd Ddu, or South Snowdon as it was named to attract tourists. There were plans for an extension to include the tourist centre of Beddgelert and even a rack railway to the summit of Snowdon, but the impoverished resources of the railway thwarted such ambitions. The Bryngwyn branch closed in January 1914, and passenger operations had ceased on the remainder of the route by 1916, although some freight continued.

Further south was to be found the Portmadoc, Beddgelert & South Snowdon Railway. This railway also had aspirations to connect Rhyd Ddu with

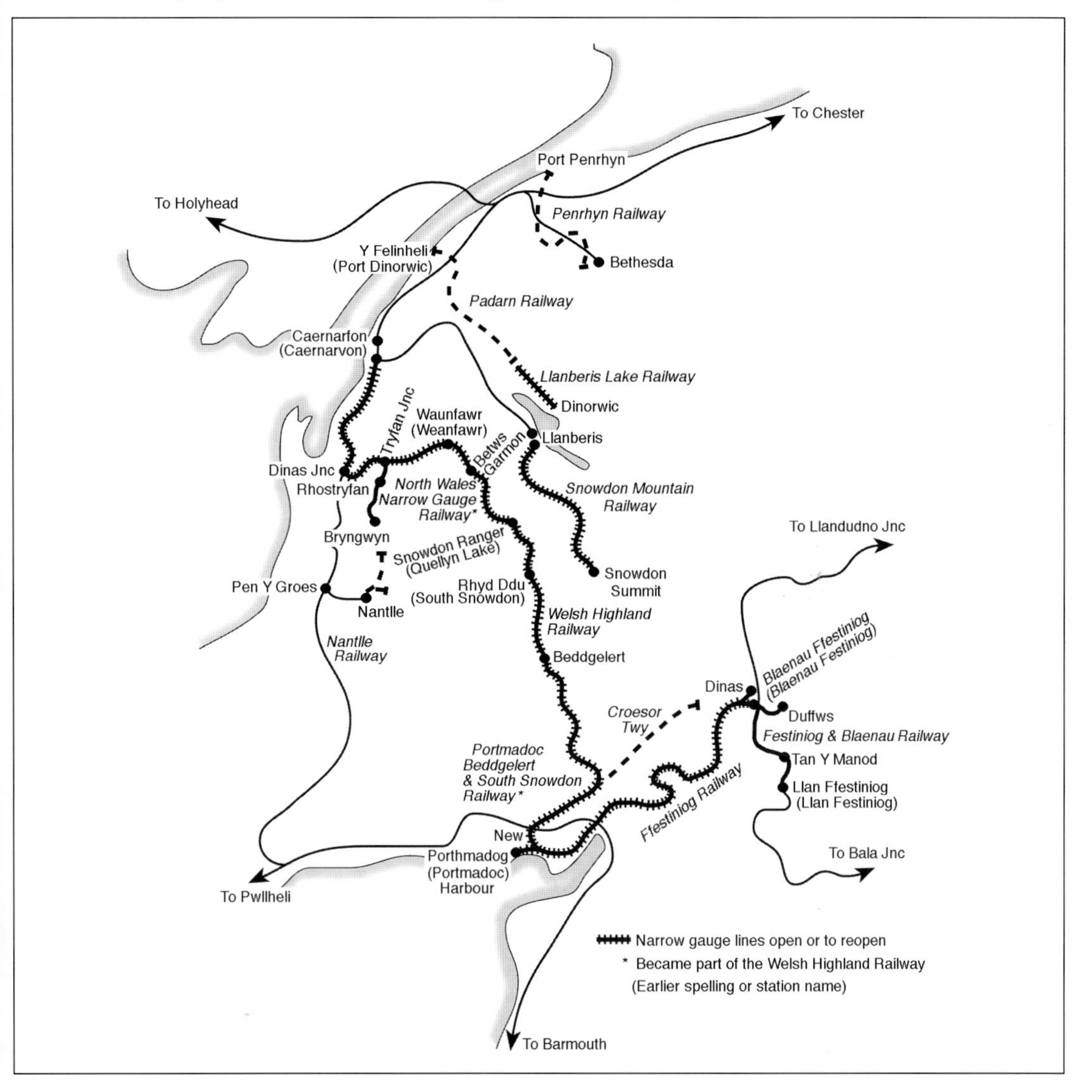

Beddgelert and Portmadoc (as it was then spelt), and a number of uncompleted sections of line were built, totalling almost 5 miles. There were even plans for electrification, but again financial difficulties frustrated such plans.

In 1922 government finance was made available to help the economy of the region, and the Welsh Highland Railway (Light Railway) Co was established with the aim of revitalising the area. The existing lines were modified and extended, and the new line created ran from Dinas, on the Bangor to Afon Wen main line, through the spectacular south Snowdon area, to Portmadoc. It was opened throughout in June 1923. Unfortunately, almost as soon as it was completed, the general economic situation worsened. The line was not a financial success, and in 1927 an Official Receiver was called in.

Colonel Stephens, as chairman of both the Welsh Highland and Festiniog railways, made economies. Regrettably, the cost-saving measures introduced eventually resulted in an infrequent and sometimes unreliable service, further reducing revenue. By 1931 passenger trains ran on just three days a week, during the summer only, with freight trains being equally infrequent.

In 1934, in order to keep services going, the Festiniog Railway leased, for £1, the Welsh Highland Railway. At this time the combined venture was not a success, and the Welsh Highland line closed to passengers at the end of the 1936 season and to all traffic the following year. Furthermore, the association of the two railways had seriously weakened the Festiniog's finances. By 1941 most of the Welsh Highland track had been removed for the war effort, although some short sections survived until the early 1950s.

A revival came from the Ffestiniog Railway again in 1995. The railway was given powers to take over from the Welsh Highland's Official Receiver, in whose hands the original route had survived. A new railway is being built to run all the way from Caernarfon to Porthmadog (as now spelt), creating a 25-mile-long 1ft 11½in-guage system. The first section from Caernarfon to Dinas opened in 1997 (see *Lost Lines — LMR*), was extended over the former Welsh Highland Railway to Waunfawr in 2000, and is now heading south towards Porthmadog.

Rheilffordd Eryri (the Welsh Highland Railway) and the Welsh language have seen a revival, but the area south of Snowdon still has many narrow-gauge remains. The Bryngwyn branch and some uncompleted sections of the Portmadoc, Beddgelert & South Snowdon Railway, together with parts of the Croesor Tramway, are likely to remain lost lines.

Right: Dinas Junction, on the former Welsh Highland Railway, showing the shed, which contained the line's Baldwin. The water tank and the signalbox, which was out of use, can also be seen in this view taken on 31 August 1926. *H. C. Casserley*

Below left: North Wales Narrow Gauge Railway locomotive *Russell*. The 2-6-2T Hunslet engine was built in 1906 and is seen here in its original non-cut-down form, at Dinas shed. Behind *Russell* is *Gowrie*, a Hunslet 0-6-4T single Fairlie, which was also purchased by the North Wales Narrow Gauge Railway. *Gowrie* was sold in 1918, thus dating this view to between 1906 and 1918. *Ian Allan Library*

Below: Moel Tryfan on the former Welsh Highland Railway. The locomotive was built at the Vulcan Foundry in 1877 and was inherited from the North Wales Narrow Gauge Railway. The locomotive is seen here in a cut-down form for use on the Festiniog Railway. It returned to Boston Lodge, on the closure of passenger services on the Welsh Highland Railway, in 1936. It was never to steam again, and was cut up for scrap as late as 1954. *Ian Allan Library*

Left: The Festiniog Railway's *Welsh Pony*, dating from 1867, ventures onto the former Welsh Highland Railway and is seen here with a train from Portmadoc at Beddgelert in June 1925. Passengers could wait for up to 50 minutes at this station, and as a consequence more photographs were taken here than at any other station on the line. *Ian Allan Library*

Below left: Brnyfelin Bridge over the River Glaslyn in the Aberglaslyn Pass, seen here soon after completion in 1923. The 70ft girder-span bridge remains to this day. *Ian Allan Library*

Above right: In 1923 the Welsh Highland Railway purchased a Baldwin 4-6-0T from the WD for £240. Dating from 1917, it was bulkier than other locomotives on the railway, and is seen here at Portmadoc. The locomotive was not a great success on the line, and was scrapped in 1941. *Ian Allan Library*

Centre right: Rudimentary facilities at Portmadoc 'New' station, with Beddgelert siding visible beyond. The cost to the Welsh Highland Railway for its trains to cross the GWR main line led to the construction, in 1933, of this further 'New' station to the north of the original 1923 Welsh Highland station at Portmadoc. Passengers were subsequently forced to walk over the main line that separated the two Welsh Highland stations. *Ian Allan Library*

Below right: One of the shorter tunnels in the Aberglaslyn Pass, seen here in September 1987. The unlined tunnel was built to a loading gauge that would permit electrification of the line. The tunnel sees a return to railway use, as part of the reconstruction of the new Welsh Highland Railway — Rheilffordd Eryri. *Author*

12 Surrey Border & Camberley

In September 1939 the fledgling Surrey Border & Camberley Railway was closed, on the outbreak of World War 2. Although of a miniature 10¼ in gauge, it deserves a mention by virtue of its ambitions to become a major railway.

The first section of line from Farnborough Green opened in July 1938, with the 2-mile route to Camberley being completed soon after. Five platforms and a 60ft by 40ft glass overall roof distinguished the miniature terminus at Farnborough that came complete with a public announcement system and train indicator boards.

It was, by any standards, an impressive line, with engine sheds and workshops. It ran all year round, trains were run until 3am for special events, and snowploughs were on occasion required to keep the line open during the winter. Commuters used the line; there were enclosed Pullman coaches and even slip coaches serving intermediate stations.

Nearly 50 sets of points and elaborate signalling and telegraph systems were provided, but, despite this, on one occasion there was a head-on collision on a single-line section. Considerable damage was caused to one of the locomotives involved, although there were no serious casualties.

From 1939 all stations were electrically lit, fares reduced and trains accelerated. Although passenger loadings were lighter than anticipated, the railway was still in its infancy, and much advertising was

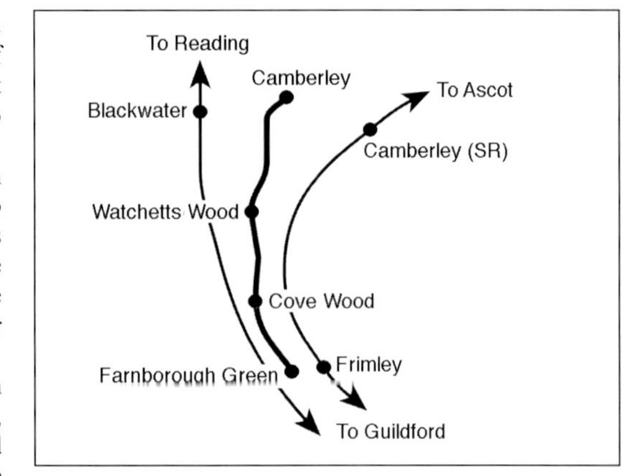

undertaken to make the public aware of its presence.

Such a substantial system had stretched resources and shortly after opening the line ran into financial difficulties. Plans for expansion were curtailed, additional loans were required and debts mounted. In

Below: Silver Jubilee, a 4-6-2 locomotive dating from 1934, takes water at the Farnborough Green terminus in 1939. The site is now part of an office complex, but the fir trees adjoining the main Guildford to Reading line, to the rear of the view, remain. *Bucknall Collection*

September 1939 World War 2 began. The line closed for the duration, but in November it was declared bankrupt. Much of the stock, together with some of the track, was removed, and by 1943 most of the track and remaining stock had gone.

The covered terminus at Farnborough Green was turned into a greenhouse, but in 1951 the company which owned it was dissolved, and gradually almost all traces of the line were lost under roads and new development in the area. Today, very few remains of the railway are to be found, but most of the locomotives still survive on other miniature lines, either in Britain or abroad. The line ran for just over a year before World War 2 brought it to a premature end. Had it survived the war, it would have been an unrivalled attraction in the area.

Right: Farnborough Green station with 2-6-0+0-6-2 Garratt No 4012, built by Kitson & Co in 1938, waiting to depart for Camberley in 1939. The powerful locomotive could haul a hundred passengers. One of the 'Pullman' coaches is also to be seen; entry to the 10¼ in-gauge coach was via the roof! The miniature Garratt was eventually shipped to Europe after World War 2.
Bucknall Collection

Below: Silver Jubilee crosses the River Blackwater in 1939, near Cove Wood. The locomotive was renamed and shipped to Scotland in 1942, after closure of the line. The rural wooded scene has been replaced by a business park and motorway interchange. Remains of the line have been obliterated.
Bucknall Collection

13 Camber casualty

World War 2 resulted in the loss of the distinctive little line from Rye to Camber. The 2½-mile, 3ft-gauge Rye & Camber Tramway ran on private land along the sandy shore of the Rother estuary, on the South Coast. The main terminus, on the southeast extremity of Rye, had the words 'Tram Station' proudly painted in huge white letters on its roofs, but this was more of a leisure railway than a tramway.

The line opened as far as Camber in July 1895, where a ferry provided a link to Rye Harbour. Later, the station was renamed 'Golf Links' and the line was extended to Camber Sands, opening in July 1908. Colonel Stephens was involved with the tramway, both in its construction and as locomotive superintendent.

The line was well used in summer and the tramway's two carriages were, on occasions, augmented by two open trucks, converted for passenger use. In winter, trains were cut back to Golf Links and used mainly by golfers. Subsidies from the golf club ended in 1925, and the following year all winter services ceased. A rival bus service began and, as more golfers used their own cars, economies were introduced on the line. A petrol tractor took over most of the services from 1925 and *Victoria*, one of the two steam locomotives, was sold for scrap. Golf Links station was reduced to the status of a halt in 1935. Although the finances of the line deteriorated, prudent measures meant that just one man was able to run the tramway in its later days.

A small amount of freight, mainly in the form of sand, was also conveyed on the line. Indeed, a separate narrow-gauge mineral railway, extracting shingle, operated in the area, and once crossed under the tramway.

The line remained independent at the amalgamation of railway companies in 1923. The Southern Railway examined the feasibility of taking over the route and adding it to its network, but the cost of conversion to standard gauge, together with the physical difficulties of connecting to the existing main-line system at Rye, put paid to the idea.

As the 1939 summer season was coming to an end, World War 2 was declared. The Admiralty feared a German invasion of this part of the South Coast, and in 1940 the line was requisitioned; a pier was built on the River Rother at Golf Links, and the northern part of the line was operated to facilitate construction of the pier and other defences in the area. Consideration was even given to re-gauging and linking the line with the nearby 15in-gauge Romney, Hythe & Dymchurch Railway, which had its own armoured train.

Although there was no land invasion, the buildings at Rye and rolling stock ended up in a poor state of repair. It was therefore decided not to reopen the railway once hostilities had ended. Most of the track and remaining stock were scrapped in 1946 and the company was wound up in 1949.

Some of the old railway infrastructure lingers on. Although all traces of the stations at Rye and Camber have gone, the lightly-constructed corrugated-iron intermediate station at Golf Links remains; a respectable length of the lightweight track also exists at this point.

Above: Both the Bagnall-built 2-4-0Ts *Camber* and *Victoria*, at Camber station prior to World War 1. *Victoria* had already lost her name, and was sold in 1926. *Camber* was subsequently little used, but survived World War 2, only to be scrapped in 1947. *Ian Allan Library*

Below: Close-up of *Camber*, in green livery, at Rye. Bagnall built both engines for the line's opening in 1895. The driving wheels of *Victoria* were 2ft in diameter and those of *Camber* a mere 1ft 9in. *LPC*

Left: Victoria, a Bagnall-built 2-4-0T dating from 1895, stands at Rye station in blue livery. Also visible are the railway's two enclosed coaches, one of which offered first and third class. At peak times, open trucks converted to passenger use were pressed into service. *LPC*

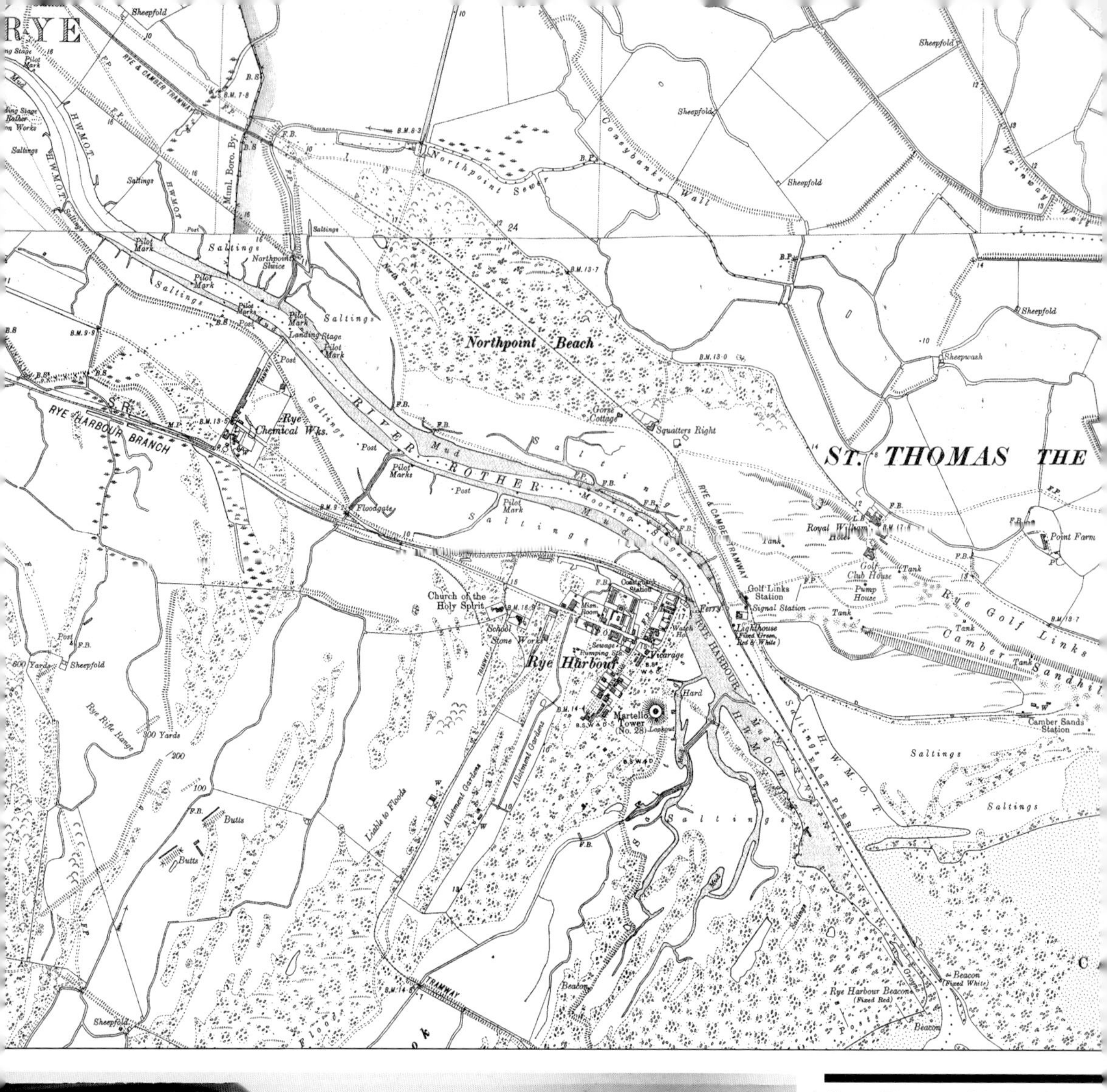

Above: The route of the Rye & Camber Tramway in 1930. *Crown copyright*

Left: Hardly having the same charm as the steam locomotives, a four-wheel Simplex petrol tractor, purchased in 1925 from the Kent Construction Co, heads a train at Camber. *LPC*

Right: The 3ft-gauge track, near Golf Links, was cemented into a roadway during World War 2, giving it the appearance of a tramway for the first time. This section still remains, and this view was taken in September 1999. *Author's collection*

Above: The petrol engine and both enclosed coaches wait to depart from Rye. The driving cab was enlarged after purchase, but the general consensus was that the engine resembled a lawnmower. The frame of one of the bogie coaches used on the line, dating from 1895, is to be found at Amberley Museum in West Sussex. *Real Photographs*

Below: Golf Links station was opened in 1895 and became an unstaffed halt in 1935. During World War 2 the Admiralty requisitioned the line and the passing-loop was rebuilt. A siding was also added to provide a link to a new pier built out into the River Rother. The station was lightly constructed, from corrugated iron, but still remains intact 60 years after closure, as seen here in September 1999. *Author's collection*

14 Ffestiniog — the wilderness years

In 1939 the summer-only passenger services on the Festiniog Railway ended with the outbreak of World War 2, although some slate traffic continued to use the line. When hostilities ceased, the railway simply had not the funds to get its track and coaches in a fit state to recommence passenger services. The once-celebrated Festiniog Railway was forced to close at the start of the quarry holidays, in August 1946.

Arguably the most famous narrow-gauge line, the 1ft 11½in (60cm) Festiniog Railway (as originally spelt and built in 1836) ran 13¼miles from the Blaenau Festiniog area to Portmadoc. James Spooner undertook the construction of the route, while his son Charles took the line into the steam age and made improvements that enabled slate to run by gravity, from over 700ft above sea level at the quarries, to the coastal wharves. Built as a mineral railway, this was the first narrow-gauge line to introduce steam, in 1863. The spectacular scenery attracted tourists and the line provided the first official passenger service in 1865, and the first narrow-gauge bogie coaches from 1873.

At its peak the railway found that it was unable to handle the volume of traffic that developed. Well over 1,000 slate wagons were in use, and in 1869 it was decided to double the track. However, at the same time it was shown that articulated Fairlie engines could safely haul substantial loads on steep gradients and round sharp curves on such a narrow gauge. The power and superiority of the Fairlie 'double engines' transformed the operation of the railway. Consequently the expense of doubling the track was found to be unnecessary.

Today's Ffestiniog Railway is most certainly not a lost line, but it very nearly was. The slate industry was in decline and the wharves were unable to handle the increasing size of vessels. The closure in 1946 could have been the end — in 1950 the Festiniog Railway applied for an Abandonment Order from the Ministry of Transport. Fortunately this was refused, and the line remained in a moribund state. Part of the route was even flooded by water to form a reservoir, and the prospect of reopening looked ever bleaker.

Happily, the railway came back from the wilderness years. In 1954, enthusiasts, having seen what was possible on the Talyllyn Railway, reopened the first section of line. A deviation around the reservoir was

Left: A passenger train stands at Duffws station, prior to its closure to passengers in 1930. Winter passenger services were also withdrawn over the whole line in October of that year. The former station is now in use as public toilets. *LPC*

Above: Blaenau Ffestiniog stations, with the ex-LMS on the left and the Festiniog Railway station to the right, in August 1951. Note the point levers, signal and water column. An air of desolation pervades the scene, but a 650yd section of the railway was still used by local quarries, to gain access to the former LMS and GWR main-line yards. *R. Simpson*

Right: The derelict double-track level road crossing at Blaenau Ffestiniog on 22 August 1965, looking towards Tan-y-Bwlch. This was one of the few such level crossings on Britain's mainly single-track narrow-gauge lines. *P. Plowman*

later built and the railway had returned to Blaenau Ffestiniog by 1982, an achievement befitting the railway's original pioneering spirit.

Some sections of the old Festiniog Railway remain lost, including a number of mineral links. On the passenger side, the original upper terminus at Dinas closed in 1870. Haford-y-Llyn closed in 1872, the link to Duffws finally closed in 1930 and Moelwyn Halt by 1924. The old Moelwyn Tunnel is also closed. The 730yd tunnel was cut through solid rock, and opened in 1842.

In 1964 I wrote a rather fanciful article for the school magazine about the Moelwyn Tunnel. It mentioned a curse on the tunnel and even the secrets of eternal life. An extract is reported below:

'In 1839 tenders were put out to build the tunnel, to a width of four paces and twice the height of a well-set-up fellow. The contractor was very short and the tunnel turned out to be only 8ft wide and 9ft high, which caused great inconvenience to the railway.'

Certainly, the narrow bore of the original horse tunnel was a curse to the railway when steam was introduced; *Russell*, even when cut down, became stuck in the tunnel. As to the secrets of eternal life, although the tunnel is lost, the Ffestiniog Railway appears to have this gift.

Above: A view near Tanygrisiau, on 22 August 1965, looking towards Portmadoc. The line was blocked by rocks, which delayed the reopening of this section. Remedial action to prevent further rock-falls onto the line was required in this area. In May 1982 the line was reopened and trains once again ran along this section of railway. *P. Plowman*

Left: The northern portal of the Moelwyn Tunnel, exposed here on 22 August 1965 at a time when the Tanygrisiau Reservoir was low. The railway opposed the scheme to flood this part of the line, but in 1956 the line in this area was compulsorily purchased for the reservoir scheme. A 2½-mile deviation was subsequently constructed as a means of reopening the entire railway. *P. Plowman*

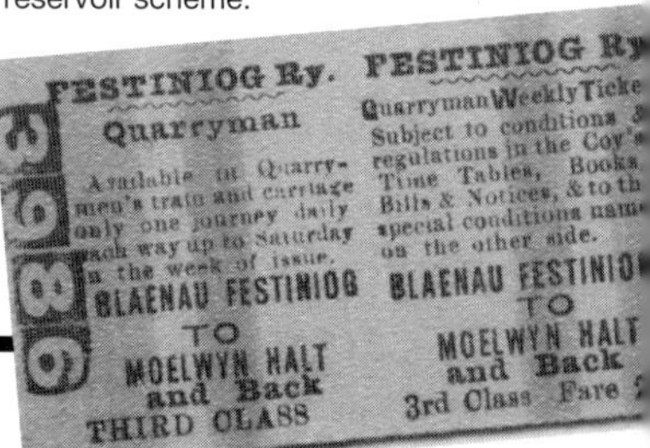

Right: Minffordd station in 1948. The tracks are still there, under the vegetation. The square patches of light are from holes in the roof of the platform shelter. Passenger trains were restored to the station in 1956. *J. Griffiths*

Centre right: Dereliction at Boston Lodge in 1953. This shows the enormous task that was required of the early preservationists to return the railway to use from its abandoned state. *M. Ware*

Below right: Boston Lodge works on 29 September 1957, with 0-4-4-0T Fairlie *Merddin Emrys*, dating from 1879, and 0-4-0ST *Prince*, dating from 1864. Both locomotives had been withdrawn in 1946. The Fairlie had not at this time been overhauled and put back in running order, but the great revival from the wilderness years had begun. *Ivo Peters*

15 Corris contraction

In August 1948 floods resulted in the end of services on the Corris line, when the embankment approach to the bridge over the River Dyfi was damaged.

This 2ft 3in-gauge line originally ran from the slate quarries at Upper Corris and Aberllefenni, to Machynlleth and onto the quay at Derwenlas, on the Dyfi estuary. The line opened in 1859 and was known as the Corris, Machynlleth & River Dovey Tramroad. The railway was engineered by Arthur Causton, and was built on a less grand scale than was the Festiniog Railway. Horses and gravity operated the route until 1864, when the title was changed to the Corris Railway.

The section to Derwenlas, to the west of Machynlleth, was the first to close, once the Aberystwyth & Welsh Coast Railway opened a standard-gauge line in 1864 and duplicated this part of the narrow-gauge route. Much of the remaining route ran parallel to the road as it snaked its way up the beautiful Dulas Valley. Although not a road tramway, in 1878 the line became part of the Imperial Tramways Co of Bristol. The following year, after upgrading the track, the first locomotives arrived, although the branches to the quarries at Aberllefenni and Ratgoed were to remain horse-worked.

After some opposition, an Act was passed in 1883 to allow passengers to be officially carried. At first services operated over the 5-mile section between Machynlleth and Corris, but in 1887 the services were extended 1½ miles to Aberllefenni. Tramway-type four-wheel saloons were originally provided for the services, but in later years charming observation saloons could be seen on the line to cater for the growing tourist traffic. In 1879 the railway also started to run bus services in the area.

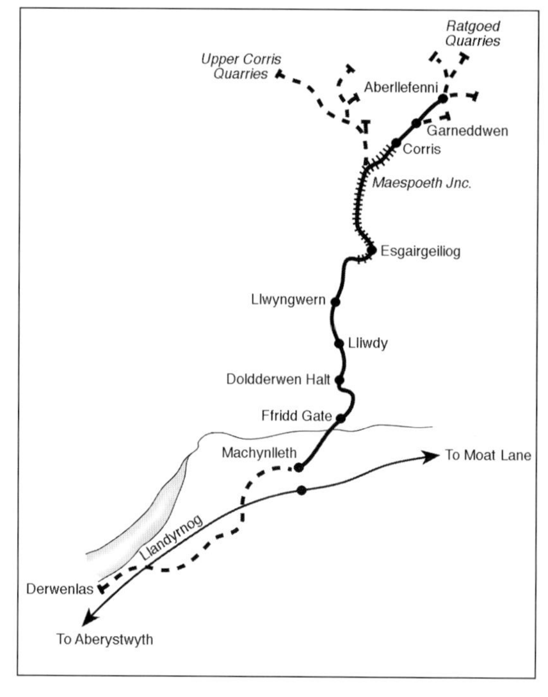

In January 1931 the line formally became part of the Great Western Railway. The GWR coveted the

Left: Corris station, seen in this view, provided shelter for the platform under the left-hand roof. Passenger services opened to this station in 1883. The loop line to the right was used mainly as a siding. The main station building has subsequently been demolished, but the stables remain and are in use as a railway museum. *LPC*

railway-operated bus services and almost immediately ceased running the railway passenger services. Some economies were made, and by 1943 the daily goods train had been reduced to a thrice-weekly service. In 1945 the line was cut back again, when the Upper Corris branch was dismantled.

In 1948 the railway was one of the few narrow-gauge routes to be nationalised. British Railways acted with similar haste to the GWR and closed the main line, in August 1948, after flooding of the River Dyfi damaged the embankment approach to the bridge north of Machynlleth. Although this incident precipitated closure, by this time freight traffic was infrequent and the future looked bleak in any event. A section of the line at the quarry at Ratgoed lasted until the early 1950s, while some quarry lines at Aberllefenni survived *in situ* until the early 1980s. More remarkably, a section is still in use at one of the slate mines.

On closure, two locomotives, Nos 3 and 4, together with a passenger coach body, found their way to the Talyllyn Railway, where, beautifully restored, they are still in operation. Much of the route remains, including the substantial station building at Machynlleth. There is a museum at the old Corris stables, and track has been re-laid between Corris and Maespoeth and Tan y coed, with plans for further extensions towards Machynlleth.

Above: Aberllefenni, deep in the Welsh mountains, was the northern passenger terminus of the Corris Railway. The station is seen here, with a Falcon-built 0-4-2ST in charge of a three-coach train. The section of line from Corris to Aberllefenni opened to passengers in 1887. *LPC*

Right: Maespoeth ground frame, seen here in the left foreground, was removed in 1940. The stone-built engine shed and workshop in the distance still remains, and is used by the Corris Railway Society in conjunction with the preserved section of line. *LPC*

Left: A two-coach passenger train hauled by No 4, a Kerr Stuart 0-4-2ST locomotive dating from 1921. The locomotive worked hard on the line, until it was taken out of service in 1947. No 4 is seen here pausing at the locomotive shed near Maespoeth Junction. *LPC*

Centre left: No 3, a 0-4-0ST built in 1878 at the Falcon Works at Loughborough for the Corris Railway. The locomotive was rebuilt in 1900 with a larger boiler, and is seen here on a train leaving Llwyngwern. The locomotive continued to be used on the Corris Railway until closure in 1948, and was sold to the Talyllyn Railway in 1951. *Bucknall Collection*

Below left: Kerr Stuart of Stoke-on-Trent built 0-4-0ST No 4 in 1921 for the Corris Railway. It is seen here at Machynlleth. The locomotive was sold to the Talyllyn Railway in 1951 and was subsequently overhauled by the Hunslet Engine Co, successor to Kerr Stuart. *Bucknall Collection*

Top right: A set of four of the attractive saloon coaches. The Metropolitan Carriage & Wagon Co Ltd provided two of the distinctive bogie coaches; the others were built partly by remodelling the original four-wheel coaches. All but one of the railway's eight bogie coaches were in use until 1930, when passenger services were abruptly withdrawn by the GWR. *LPC*

ABERLLEFENI (Merioneth) 225 miles. No through fares From London as to Machynlleth, thence 35 minutes, about 3 times daily.

CORRIS (Merioneth). 224 miles. No through fares. From London as to Machynlleth, thence 25 minutes, 3 times daily

Above: Service frequency in 1930.

Above: A double-headed seven-coach train (plus covered van) crosses the original bridge over the River Dyfi. This postcard was dated April 1905 and sent to Bridge Street, in Corris. A more substantial bridge replaced the slender wooden structure in 1906. *Bucknall Collection*

Right: The second bridge over the Dyfi was far more substantial. Dating from 1906, it had four metal girder-spans, each 172ft across. The new bridge was built to withstand a considerable increase in river flow. Nevertheless, serious floods damaged the embankment approach in August 1948, resulting in the closure of the railway. *LPC*

Left: Although the Corris main line ceased to run after 1948, slate was still brought down from the quarries to the works at Aberllefenni by rail. Here a wagon loaded with slate, with a brakeman aboard, is towed down to the works below by a tractor. This highly-unusual railway working was noted on 5 September 1962. *J. White*

Centre left: The original passenger station at Corris has been demolished. However, the new Corris station, seen here in July 1999, is in the same area as the original. The track extends ¾ mile to Maespoeth, with a 2-mile further extension planned to open in 2001. *Author*

Above: One of the Corris coaches has been restored on the Talyllyn Railway, and is seen here at Tywyn in June 1999. No 17, dating from 1898, ended up in a garden at Gobowen before arriving at Tywyn; following restoration, it re-entered service in 1961, finished in the brown Corris Railway livery. The original wooden slatted seats have sensibly been provided with cushions. *Author*

Left: The Corris Railway station at Machynlleth was located a short distance to the north of the GWR station, on the edge of the town. A new station was opened in 1907; this was a substantial stone affair, and the main booking office remains today, as can be seen from this July 1999 view. *Author*

16 Abandoned at Ashover

March 1950 saw the final freight trains trundle over the Ashover Light Railway. This was the last public narrow-gauge passenger line in England to close. It had also been the last significant light railway to open in Britain, commencing freight services in 1924 and passenger services the following year. The 7½-mile line ran from limestone and fluorspar quarries at Ashover to works at Clay Cross, where there were also interchange facilities with the LMS. Other branches were proposed, but not built.

The railway was constructed economically, using surplus World War 1 material from France. As such, the line was built to a 60cm (1ft 11½in) gauge. The railway originally operated six distinctive American-built Baldwin 4-6-0T locomotives, but these were cannibalised and interchanged until only two complete examples were in full working order at the end. Various petrol and diesel tractors also worked over the line, but these were the property of the Clay Cross Company.

The Clay Cross to Stretton section followed very broadly the Midland main line, but it was built far more economically, with heavy inclines. The route from Stretton to Ashover Butts ran through attractive countryside on the edge of the Derbyshire Peak District. The line opened to passengers in April 1925 and over 5,000 were carried in the first week. Four saloon coaches were built on ex-WD underframes, while eight partly-open bogie coaches, from the Wembley Exhibition of 1926, were later added to the stock.

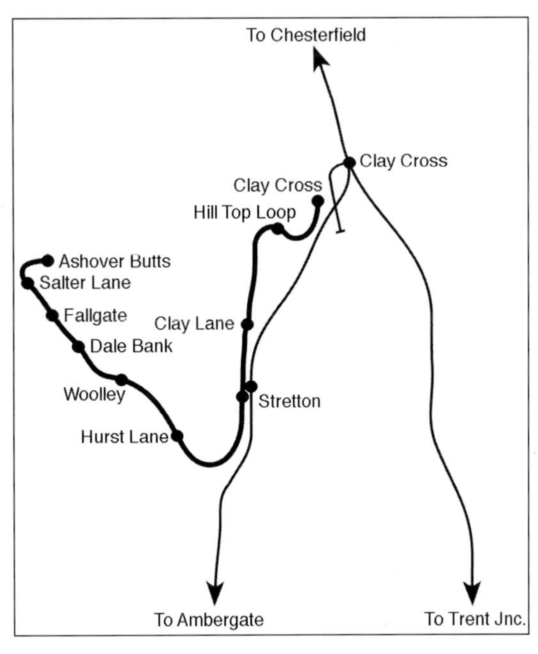

Despite the considerable number of halts provided on the line, inevitably a rival bus service was established, and the daily passenger service ceased in September 1930. A summer-only service continued until 1936, thus ending just over 10 years of passenger operation, although passenger specials were run until 1947.

Right: Passengers wait at Ashover Butts station. The wooden station buildings were to a standard design used on the line. Much of the route of the old line in this area is still evident in the attractive Derbyshire landscape. *SLS*

Left: Ashover Butts; a single-coach passenger train turns using part of the reversing triangle on the approach to the terminus. The triangle also provided a spur to the quarry. *LPC/SLS*

Below: Hummy, a Baldwin 4-6-0T locomotive built originally for the War Department in 1917. It is seen here in good condition during the early days of the railway, with two coaches on the reversing triangle at Ashover Butts. The locomotive was scrapped in 1951. *Real Photographs*

Left: Peggy, a 4-6-0T, also built by Baldwin in 1917 for use in France, is seen here on the Ashover line. The locomotive was scrapped in 1951, but one of the nameplates survives at the Tywyn museum. *Bucknall Collection*

A stock of over 70 bogie wagons was at one time provided for the freight services. One of the transporter wagons from the Leek & Manifold Railway was also purchased on the closure of that line, but was not a success. However, freight continued until March 1950, when British Railways' ballast contract was terminated. By then most of the remaining equipment was in a poor state of repair; the track, in particular, was in a rough condition, as it was originally intended only for limited military use, and a start was made on dismantling the line later in the year.

Today, remains can still be found, and several sections of the route traced. Near the quarry at Ashover Butts part of the points of the turning triangle lingers on. The platform edge at Salter Lane can just about be made out. At Fallgate, the wooden station building remains, together with some track into one of the smaller quarries. At Clay Cross one of the original coaches, with its longitudinal wooden seating, still exists and is in use as a pavilion for a bowling club.

Above right: An attractive pose for the camera of a one-coach passenger train on the line near Ashover, during the early days of the railway. The acetylene headlamp on the front of the engine is an interesting feature of this particular view. *Bucknall Collection*

Centre right: The Ashover Railway station at Stretton was adjacent to the LMS station, on the Midland main line. As such, it was once the most important intermediate stop, and Ashover trains would be held for up to 20 minutes awaiting connections. Nevertheless, limited facilities are seen at the closed station when this view, looking north to Clay Cross, was taken on 14 May 1949. The level crossing, seen in the distance, was over the Mansfield to Matlock road. *T. Wassell*

Right: The sad remains of the former Baldwin locomotive *Bridget*, seen here on 14 May 1949 outside Clay Cross shed. The locomotive was withdrawn from service in 1947 and cannibalised for spares; the remains were finally scrapped in 1951. *T. Wassell*

Left: Fallgate passenger station buildings, wooden-built in traditional Ashover Light Railway style. The building still remained in June 1999, when viewed here, long after many more substantial railway structures had disappeared. *Author*

Below left: Tracks running into Milltown Quarry remain set in the road near Fallgate, as is apparent from this June 1999 picture. The rural tranquillity of today belies the fact that, at one time, this area was the centre of much industrial activity. *Author*

Below right: One of the remaining original Gloucester-built Ashover coaches. This vehicle was to be found at the Clay Cross Bowling Club in June 1999. The coach still retains its longitudinal wooden seats. The four original coaches of this design were all of single-class layout. *Author*

17 An Irish interlude

The closure of the last narrow-gauge passenger line in Ireland was seen in 1961. The roads in parts of Ireland were not good; there was also rural poverty and a number of lines far outlived those in England. Unlike the range of narrow gauges in England and Wales, the 500 miles or so of Irish narrow-gauge passenger lines all had the same 3ft gauge. Even though a consistent gauge was used, the stock itself was not all of a standard nature, and could not always be easily interchanged on different lines. Sadly all the original lines are now lost.

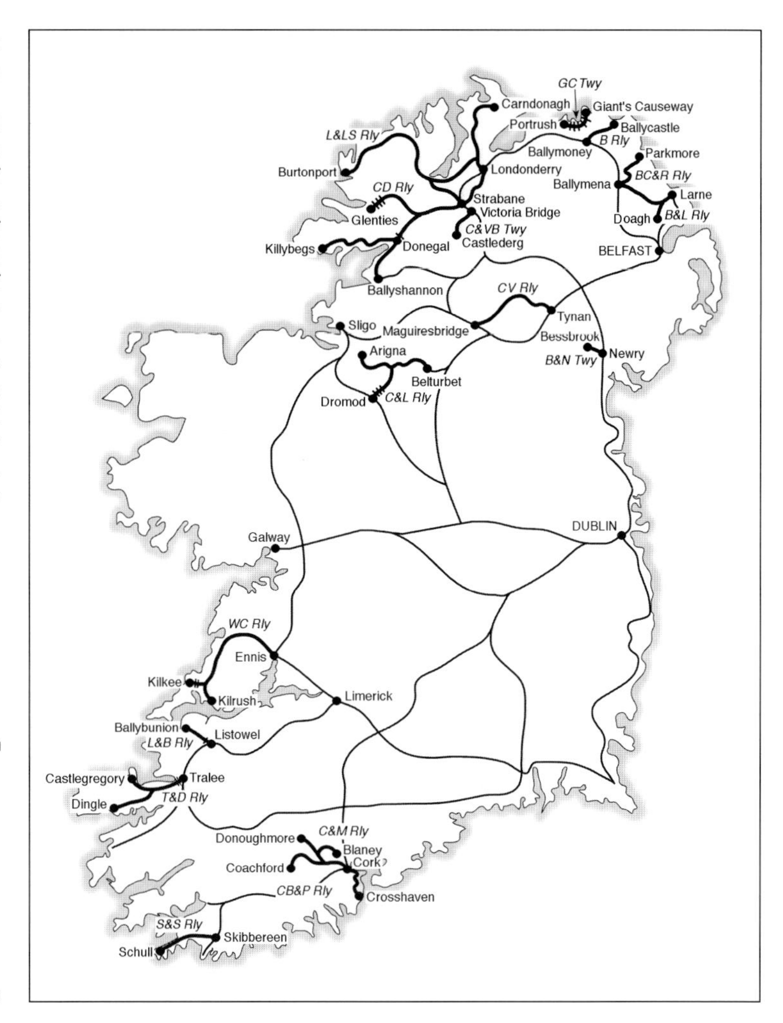

Below: No 4 was the largest locomotive used on the Clogher Valley Railway. It was originally built in 1904 for the Castlederg & Victoria Bridge Tramway. On the closure of that line in 1933, the 2-6-2T was purchased by the Clogher Valley Railway. It is seen here on a passenger working at Aughnacloy in 1937. *Ian Allan Library*

Left: A tram runs along the Giant's Causeway Tramway, on the Antrim coast, at Dunluce Castle in 1890. A 6-mile electric service between Portrush and Bushmills began in November 1883 and was extended to the Giant's Causeway in 1887. The exposed electric conductor-rail can be seen in this view, with a gap for the field entrance. An electric overhead wire replaced the live rail in 1899. The original line survived until 1949. *Ian Allan Library*

Bottom: The Clogher Valley Railway ran some 37 miles, from Maguiresbridge to Tynan. Both termini provided broad-gauge connections to the former GNR(I). Nos 3 and 6 are seen here with a pig train at Aughnacloy in 1937; both 0-4-2T locomotives were built by Sharp Stewart in 1887. This was a mainly roadside line, and the locomotives were fitted with tramway skirts. The line closed to all traffic in 1941. *Ian Allan Library*

Ulster Transport Authority

In Northern Ireland, of the independent companies, the first major closure came in 1933 with the end of services on the 7¼-mile roadside Castlederg & Victoria Bridge Tramway. The 37-mile Clogher Valley Railway followed this in 1941, despite the road fuel shortages that existed during World War 2. Electrification was not to save the 3-mile Bessbrook & Newry Tramway, which closed in 1948, while the 8-mile electric Giant's Causeway Tramway remained in use, mainly for summer tourists, until 1949.

In 1903 a number of narrow-gauge lines in the north of Ireland had become part of the Midland Railway of England. By 1924 they became part of the Northern Counties Committee of the London Midland & Scottish Railway. Consequently, as an early economy, the 16½-mile Ballymena, Cushendall & Red Bay line was closed to passengers by the LMS in 1930, although a section remained open for freight until 1940.

In 1948 the Ulster Transport Authority (UTA) took over the remaining narrow-gauge lines in Northern Ireland, and lost little time in ending narrow-gauge operations in County Antrim. The last section of the once 30½-mile Ballymena & Larne Railway, which until 1931 had run non-stop corridor-coach boat trains connecting with LMS sailings at Larne, was closed in July 1950. The 16¼-mile Ballycastle Railway succumbed at the same time.

GIANT'S CAUSEWAY and PORTRUSH.—Giant's Causeway, Portrush, and Bush Valley.
From Portrush at 10*40 mrn., and 3 15 aft. **From Bushmills** at 9 55 mrn. and 2 35 aft.
* If there be three or more **Passengers** the 10 40 mrn. will run through to **Giant's Causeway** and return at 2 20 aft.

Above: Londonderry & Lough Swilly Railway No 10 *Richmond*, a Kerr Stuart 4-6-2T locomotive dating from 1904, is seen here with a Buncrana train, waiting to depart from Londonderry on 19 April 1948. The line closed in 1953 and the locomotive was scrapped the following year. *H. C. Casserley*

Cross-border railways

There were two lines where, after the 1921 partition of Ireland, customs formalities had to be observed at border stations. The Londonderry & Lough Swilly Railway once boasted almost 100 miles of line stretching to remote Burtonport, and the County Donegal Railways Joint Committee at one time extended to 123 miles. Both railways had separate termini at the port of Londonderry (or Derry) and served isolated areas — so remote and bleak in fact that, on occasions, rolling stock was physically blown off the track in gales. The worst incident occurred in 1925, at Owencrow Viaduct, when four passengers were killed.

The narrow-gauge operation of the Londonderry & Lough Swilly Railway dated from 1883. It was an impressive system, and in 1903 carried King Edward VII on a visit to Ireland. It also operated the massive 4-8-4Ts on its main line — at over 50 tons these were some of the heaviest and most powerful narrow-gauge locomotives in operation in the British Isles. From the late 1920s the railway saw its future in road transport, and the last 12-mile freight section, from Londonderry to Buncrana, closed in 1953.

The Donegal Railway ran from Londonderry to Strabane and on to a number of destinations in County Donegal. The network of 3ft narrow-gauge lines dated back to 1893. By 1906 the Donegal Railway was in a poor financial state and was taken over by the Great Northern Railway of Ireland and the Midland Railway of England. They formed the County Donegal Railways Joint Committee (CDRJC), with the Midland Railway being responsible for running the Londonderry to Strabane section.

The CDRJC became a real fighter, existing on meagre earnings in a sparse rural area, innovating in 1931 with the first diesel railcars and providing connecting bus services. For a time it became one of the few profitable railways in Ireland, yet the Londonderry to Strabane section was closed by the UTA in 1954 and soon losses began to increase. Track and bridges were in a deteriorating condition and in 1957 a formal application for closure was made.

The final trains ran on 31 December 1959. *Drumboe* hauled the last train, as the regular railcar was unable to cope with the crowds. The rain and the exploding detonators added to the sense of loss expressed by many on that night. The Donegal lines were lifted soon after, but not all of the stock was scrapped. Four locomotives were saved, and the Isle of Man Railway acquired railcars Nos 19 and 20.

Above: Londonderry & Lough Swilly Railway 4-8-4T No 5, dating from 1912, at Londonderry on 21 April 1948. Weighing over 50 tons, these were the heaviest narrow-gauge tank locomotives used in the British Isles. Note the old disc-type signal protecting the road crossing. *H. C. Casserley*

Left: Londonderry & Lough Swilly Railway 4-8-0 No 12, dating from 1905, with a freight train at Newtoncunningham on 17 September 1948. Once the most important intermediate point on the Letterkenny line, the station closed, along with the line, in 1953; the locomotive was scrapped the following year. *I. Wright*

Below left: A Letterkenny to Strabane railcar, No 12. The 74hp Walker diesel was built in 1934 and is seen here near Raphoe on 24 April 1953. The County Donegal Railways Joint Committee, with its 123 miles of line, was the most extensive narrow-gauge passenger system in the British Isles and the first to make regular use of diesel traction. *H. C. Casserley*

Above: Strabane interchange station, with the ex-GNR(I) broad-gauge 4-4-0 No 173 *Galtee More* on the left and County Donegal railcar No 20 on the right. The railcar was the last built for the CDRJC, entering service in 1951, and was sold to the Isle of Man Railway in 1961. This view dates from 22 April 1959, in the last year of narrow-gauge services on the CDRJC lines. *B. Wilkinson*

Centre right: The narrow-gauge bridge which once carried the County Donegal Railways Joint Committee line over the River Mourne at Strabane. Dating from 1894 and built at a cost of £2,450, it featured girder sections mounted on screw piles. The photograph shows the bridge being demolished, on 10 August 1965. *M. Yardley*

Right: Strabane station on 12 September 1968, with County Donegal 4-6-4Ts *Drumboe* (*Glenties* until 1937) in the background and *Meenglass* (*Donegal* until 1937) nearer the camera. Nasmyth Wilson built both engines in 1907. Although looking abandoned here, they eventually made it into preservation, as has a short section of the line itself. *C. Foss*

Córas Iompair Éireann

In Southern Ireland one of the most unusual lines was to be found. The 9½-mile Listowel & Ballybunion Railway opened in 1888. It was in fact a monorail, with the locomotives and stock straddling a raised running-rail. It was not a financial success and was one of the first passenger routes to close in Ireland, in 1924.

The following year narrow-gauge lines in Eire were grouped into the Great Southern Railways (GSR). The first two lines closed by the GSR were separate routes that radiated from Cork. The Cork, Blackrock & Passage Railway, originally built to the Irish standard gauge of 5ft 3in, was converted to narrow gauge in 1900 and by 1904 extended some 16 miles to Crosshaven from Cork, Albert Street. It possessed the only section of narrow-gauge double track in Ireland, but closed in 1932. The Cork & Muskerry Railway ran a 26½-mile network of lines, from Western Road in Cork to the famous Blarney Castle, Coachford and Donoughmore. It could not compete with the trams, and closed in 1934.

In 1945 the Great Southern Railways became part of Córas Iompair Éireann (CIE), and from 1958 that part of the Great Northern Railway of Ireland that ran in the Irish Republic also became part of CIE. The Schull & Skibbereen Railway, running some 15 miles between the settlements in its title, became the first of the remaining narrow-gauge lines to be closed by CIE, in 1946.

The Tralee & Dingle Railway was opened throughout in 1891. The main line ran some 31¼ miles between the towns in its title, and at Dingle the railway could boast of having the most westerly station in Europe. A 6-mile branch to Castlegregory closed in 1939. The main line closed to passengers at the same time, but freight continued until 1947. After this the line held on by a thread, with a monthly cattle train operating over the steeply-graded and rusting tracks in connection with Dingle fair. These spectacular trains ran until 1953.

The Cavan & Leitrim Railway ran some 33 miles between the standard-gauge interchange stations at Dromod and Belturbet. There was also a 15-mile branch to Arigna, which had been opened in 1888, a year after the main line. Coal was to be found at Arigna, but it was not until 1920 that the mines here were connected to the railway. Although freight traffic was still considerable, the cost of modernising the line was the main reason for its closure in 1959.

The West Clare Railway opened from Ennis to Milltown Malbay in 1887, and the South Clare Railway extended the route to Kilkee and Kilrush in 1892, providing a line of 53 miles. The CIE dieselised the line in 1952 and this prolonged its life, but it closed in 1961. Percy French wrote the famous poem *Are ye right there, Michael?* about this line, and as such it lives on in Irish folklore.

Thus ended all the original narrow-gauge passenger lines in Ireland. The extensive peat-carrying railways of Bord na Mona remain, and sections of the Cavan & Leitrim, Tralee, West Clare, Giant's Causeway and Donegal lines are preserved.

Above left: A train about to leave Skibbereen for Cork, on the Schull & Skibbereen Railway. This 15½-mile, mainly roadside line served a remote area to the west of Cork. A policy to open up remoter parts of the country meant that such lines were subsidised locally, but often reluctantly, and this line was nicknamed the 'Sick & Sore' Railway. *A. Hughes*

Above: Crossing the viaduct at Ballydehob, on the Schull & Skibbereen Railway. The viaduct was the largest engineering work on the line. The railway was hit by coal shortages and closed for a period in 1944-5, before closing completely in 1946. *A. Hughes*

Right: Tralee & Dingle Railway 2-6-0T locomotive No 8, dating from 1910, gets up steam during the last years of the railway. The line clung to life thanks to a monthly cattle train that ran until 1953. Locomotive No 5 from the railway is to be found on a stretch of preserved line at Tralee. *Ian Allan Library*

Above left: A Cavan & Leitrim Railway train on the 15-mile Arigna branch at Drumshanbo, on 10 September 1948. Arigna was the location of Ireland's only commercial coal mine, which helped keep the line in regular use up until its closure in 1959. A section of line has been preserved at Dromod. *I. Wright*

Centre left: Kilrush station on the West Clare line, with the 4.45pm to Moyasta and Kilkee standing at the platform, on 24 June 1959. New diesel railcars had been introduced in 1952, and this was to be the last narrow-gauge passenger line in Ireland to close, in 1961. A 1½-mile section has been preserved at Moyasta Junction. *D. Thompson*

Below left: The former independent St James's Gate Guinness brewery railway in Dublin once had its own 1ft 10in narrow-gauge system. No 22, an 0-4-0T built in Dublin in 1912, is seen here with the locomotive shed in the background, on 4 August 1956. The locomotive could be converted for broad-gauge use through being lowered into a specially-built standard-gauge haulage wagon. Use of steam on the system ended in 1965, and it closed a decade later. *C. Boocock*

18 A ghost on the Manx Northern

September 1968 saw the last major narrow-gauge passenger closure in the British Isles, with the loss of the 28 miles of line from Douglas to Ramsey and Peel on the Isle of Man.

The first public narrow-gauge line in the British Isles to convey passengers from the start was the Isle of Man Railway (IMR). The original line ran 11½ miles from the capital, Douglas, right across the island to Peel, and opened in July 1873. On the opening day a banner at Peel proclaimed 'Speedeilys Dan Raad Yiarn Eddy R Doolish As Port Ny Hinshey' — Manx for 'Success to the Iron Road between Douglas and Peel'. The line to Port Erin opened the following year, and, with the increased tourist trade to the island, an

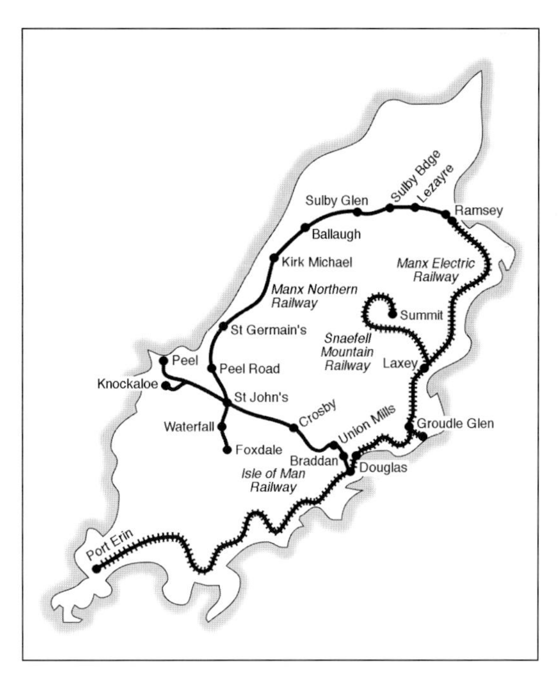

Below: Isle of Man Railway No 10 *G. H. Wood*, dating from 1905, enters the picturesque Union Mills station. The locomotive is heading the first regular passenger train, on Saturday 3 June 1967, after complete closure of the railway in November 1965. Sadly it proved to be a false dawn, and this particular line closed again in 1968. *G. Morrison*

eventual system of 46 miles of railway was developed. At its peak, over 100 passenger coaches were in stock.

The Manx Northern Railway was constructed when the Isle of Man Railway decided not to build a Ramsey branch. As a consequence, the townsfolk of Ramsey made great efforts of their own and established the independent Manx Northern Railway (MNR). This ran on the western side of the island, some 16½ miles from Ramsey to join the existing Douglas to Peel line at St John's. It was opened in September 1879, also to a 3ft gauge. Parts of the route on the western coast of the island were so exposed that carriages were turned periodically, in order to ensure that both sides weathered equally.

The 2½-mile Foxdale Railway was built primarily to serve the lead and silver mines in the Foxdale area. Opened in 1886, it was originally worked by the Manx Northern Railway, but on terms that were to lead the MNR into financial difficulties. Consequently, in 1905 the MNR was amalgamated with the IMR. As it turned out, the lead mines became exhausted, and the Foxdale line closed to passengers in 1939. General freight traffic ended in 1945, although the track was not entirely removed until the early 1970s. Finally, on the subject of lead, this was also found at Laxey and a 19in narrow-gauge industrial system existed in the area until 1929.

Whilst bus and lorry services cut into revenues, the remaining steam-operated lines continued successfully, and as late as 1956 over 1 million passengers were carried. By this time, however, tourism to the Isle of Man was decreasing, and economies had to be made. In 1960 the section of line from St John's to Peel was closed, and in 1961 ex-County Donegal railcars were obtained to run winter services. 1965 saw the entire network closed for the winter, but there was real shock when the system did not reopen for the summer of 1966. However, in 1967 the railway was leased to the Marquis of Ailsa, and a grand reopening took place. Unfortunately, the lines to Peel and to Ramsey were closed again in 1968, and the track has subsequently been lifted.

There is a ghostly tale of the sound of shunting being heard in the dead of night at Ramsey station, together with a train steaming down to the harbour branch, long after its closure. Elsewhere on the island, the spirit of the former railway can still be found. Much of the Peel line trackbed still exists as a heritage trail, and there is just a possibility that a section of line from near Peel to St John's may reopen as a park-and-ride service. Even today, there are lingering thoughts of a more extensive reopening of the line.

Other ghosts are more tangible, as sections of the island's railways are still operational. There is the steam railway from Douglas to Port Erin, the Douglas horse-trams and Manx Electric Railway, together with the Groudle Glen and Snaefell lines — all providing a remarkable living museum of narrow-gauge railways.

Left: The 3.35pm from Douglas to Ramsey passes Pulrose, just outside Douglas, behind No 8 *Fenella* on Thursday 16 June 1960. The train consists of three coaches, a van and an open wagon. This was a slow train, but a limited number of summer 'Ramsey Specials' ran from Douglas to Ramsey in an hour, providing a faster service than both the rival Manx Electric Railway and the bus service. *R. Greenwood*

Above right: Isle of Man Railway No 5 *Mona*, dating from 1874, is seen here at St John's, with a Peel to Douglas train. The train is waiting for the diesel railcar-worked service from Douglas to Peel to pass it. Since this view was taken in the 1960s, *Mona* has been out of use for many years. *B. Lane*

Centre right: Ramsey and Peel trains setting off side-by-side from St John's in June 1961. An integrated timetable was operated on the Isle of Man Railway, but boys and girls were strictly segregated on school trains. *Ivo Peters*

Below right: Isle of Man Railway No 12 *Hutchinson*, at Peel station with the afternoon train to Douglas on 27 June 1962. The station occupied the northern side of the harbour; the buildings on the left of the picture date from 1907. The original station buildings, dating from 1873, were being used as a goods shed at this time. *J. Spencer Gilks*

Above: Isle of Man Railway No 5 *Mona*, leaving St John's with a Ramsey train; No 8 *Fenella* is banking at the rear. Early in 1942 snow blocked the line and a three-coach train, double-headed and double-banked, forced its way through the drifts to reach Ramsey. *S. Basnett*

Centre left: A Ramsey to Douglas train crosses the three 60ft spans of Glen Moar Viaduct, on the now-closed Manx Northern section of line from St John's to Ramsey, in June 1961. The lattice girders were renewed in 1921. The stone piers were also about 60ft high and still remain, although the metal girders and tracks were removed in the mid-1970s. *Ivo Peters*

Below left: The three-span Glen Wyllin Viaduct, also on the closed Manx Northern section. Box girders replaced lattice girders in 1915, and were removed in the mid-1970s. This view shows the viaduct being crossed by a former County Donegal railcar. Two railcars were shipped to the island, in May 1961, after closure of the County Donegal lines. They were the most modern in the Donegal fleet and had seats for 41 passengers. They remain on the Isle of Man. *Ian Allan Library*

Right: No 1 *Sutherland* gleaming at Ramsey station on 16 May 1927. The 2-4-0T locomotive dates from 1873 and, as with all the locomotives of the former Isle of Man Railway, was built by Beyer Peacock at Manchester. A closed boiler dome and new safety-valves above the firebox have replaced the original fittings; otherwise the locomotives remain today very much as originally built. *Ian Allan Library*

Centre right: Waterfall Halt was provided for the village of Lower Foxdale, and was the only intermediate stop on the Foxdale branch. The limited facilities are viewed here on 3 July 1933. Trains stopped at the halt by request to the guard. *H. C. Casserley*

Below right: The disused Foxdale branch near Waterfall Halt, seen here on 24 August 1964. Most lead mines had closed by 1911, and the remaining weekday passenger services ceased in 1939. General freight ended after World War 2, but the spoil from the lead mines was transported away by rail, and all the track was not finally removed until the 1970s. *L. Sandler*

Left: A bleak view of the disused passenger terminus at Foxdale, with the evidence of the spoil tips from lead mining in the background. The station buildings were converted into a private residence before closure of the branch, and tickets were thenceforth issued on the train. *B. Briggs*

Centre left: The 2ft-gauge Groudle Glen Railway in April 1950, with a view of the overgrown engine shed area and one of the eight four-wheeled 'toastrack' coaches. Like part of the Isle of Man Railway, the line was to witness a revival. *H. C. Casserley*

Below left: A 19in-gauge mineral line at Laxey was steam-operated from 1875 and ran for almost a mile from lead and copper mines, until closure in 1929. The diminutive locomotive seen here was one of two, named *Ant* and *Bee*. Both were scrapped in 1935. *LPC*

19 Railways and no railways

The Festiniog Railway became a showpiece of what could be achieved with narrow gauge. Heavy loads, safe and serviceable carriages, reduced construction costs and healthy profits enthused many with the advantages of this gauge of railway.

In 1872 Robert Fairlie, whose double-articulated locomotives transformed the capabilities of narrow-gauge railways, produced a pamphlet called *Railways and No Railways*, which looked favourably on the technical and apparent financial advantages of narrow-gauge railways. As a consequence, many miles of narrow-gauge railway were laid throughout the world. Variations on Fairlie-type locomotives could be found on narrow-gauge lines as far afield as New Zealand. Narrow-gauge locomotives were also exported from British manufacturers, particularly those at Glasgow, Manchester and Newcastle, to destinations throughout the world.

Similarly, American Baldwin locomotives were imported into Britain. *Lyn* was delivered to the Lynton & Barnstaple Railway in record time. Baldwin locomotives, often ex-WD, also found their way onto the Glyn Valley, Welsh Highland and Ashover lines, and onto several mineral systems.

Over time, a huge mileage of narrow-gauge has been lost throughout the world. A few examples illustrate the scale of closures. France once had a network of some 13,000 miles of mainly metre-gauge line, whereas now only a few lines survive. In North America, about 10,000 miles of railway was at one time narrow-gauge; the last 2ft-gauge line closed in 1944 and most sections of the Denver & Rio Grande 3ft-gauge system, which was partly financed in London, had closed by 1967.

Islands were the natural home of narrow-gauge railways. Passenger systems are now extinct on islands as disparate as Antigua, Barbados, Cyprus, the Canaries, the Falklands, Malta, Newfoundland, Haiti, Oahu and Trinidad. On most other islands where narrow-gauge lines were built, the original systems have been cut back.

Some narrow-gauge equipment and rolling stock has returned to Britain, where examples of locomotives from around the world now operate on a number of preserved lines. Preserved narrow-gauge lines can also be found abroad and, in spite of the losses, a huge variety of narrow-gauge systems, many in their original working condition, remains throughout the world.

Right: British locomotives were exported from the Hunslet Engine Co at Leeds to the Sierra Leone Railway in West Africa. One of the last built in 1954 was returned to Britain in 1975, after the closure of the entire 320-mile system, to work on the preserved Welshpool & Llanfair Light Railway. The 2-6-2T is seen at Llanfair in July 1999. *Author*

Left: Temple Meads freight yard at Bristol, once a bastion of the broad gauge, was home in 1998 to 3ft 6in-gauge ex-Rhodesian Railways 4-8-0 No 930, returned from Africa. In theory the 7ft gauge was superior to narrow gauge, but in practice narrow gauge became much more widespread throughout the world. *Author*

Centre left: Beyer-Garratt exported narrow-gauge engines to the South African Railways. The 211-ton, 4-8-2+2-8-4 Garratts were some of the most powerful narrow-gauge steam locomotives built, and allowed the full potential of narrow-gauge railways to be realised. No 2352 is seen here, back at Manchester, where it was originally built in 1929. *Author's collection*

Bottom left: Islands were home to many narrow-gauge lines. Here a substantial bridge, constructed in 1917, spans a ravine near El Arenal in Majorca. Until 1964 the bridge carried the 3ft (90cm)-gauge Palma-Santanyi line. Much of this line was supplied with signalling equipment from Ransomes & Rapier of Ipswich. *Author*

Below right: Abandoned tunnel in the Aberglaslyn Pass? In fact this is an abandoned unlined tunnel on the 3ft 3in (100cm)-gauge line that until 1957 led to the monastery at Montserrat in Spain. The disused tunnel is seen here in September 1989. *Author*

20 Industrial deadlines

At one time, narrow-gauge railway lines could be found at almost any industrial complex. The systems ranged from a few yards of track, such as at Snape Maltings in Suffolk, to over 100 miles of line at the Royal Arsenal Railway in London. It would be impossible to cover the countless systems that developed and have since closed in a single book. Some of the more extensive lost industrial, military and mineral narrow-gauge lines are outlined in the next few chapters.

Great works

The London & North Western Railway's Crewe works saw raw materials roll in at one end and completed locomotives roll out at the other. From 1862 a 1ft 6in-gauge railway was developed to facilitate this transformation, and an extensive system evolved at the works. At one point the narrow-gauge line crossed a suspension bridge over the standard-gauge railway, in order to reach the main-line station. Although the first diesel to run on the LMS was purchased for this system in 1930, the railway was cut back shortly after and ceased operation in 1932, following the closure of the steel-making section of the works. Most remains had gone by the early 1980s, but *Pet*, one of the small 0-4-0ST locomotives used on the system, has been preserved.

In 1887 the Lancashire & Yorkshire Railway installed a 1ft 6in-gauge system at its Horwich works. An eventual 7½ miles of line was employed in the iron and steel foundry and in conveying materials from shop to shop around the works. The attractive 0-4-0ST locomotives used were lined out in LYR livery. *Wren*, the sole survivor of eight engines built between 1887 and 1901, has been preserved. The

Above: Pet was one of the rather utilitarian-looking 0-4-0ST narrow-gauge engines designed by John Ramsbottom. It was built in 1865 for the internal 1ft 6in-gauge line which, until its closure in 1932, served Crewe Works. This particular engine was withdrawn in 1929, but survived the cutter's torch to reach preservation as part of the National Collection. *Ian Allan Library*

Left:
Wren was the last survivor of eight 0-4-0ST engines built between 1887 and 1901 and used on the 1ft 6in-gauge system at Horwich Works. The locomotive is seen here on 15 April 1956. It was withdrawn from service in 1962, with the distinction of being BR's smallest steam locomotive; closure of the Horwich system followed soon after. The locomotive was subsequently preserved. *G. Morrison*

system closed in 1962 and Horwich works itself closed in 1983.

A narrow-gauge steam-operated railway was also to be found at Beyer Peacock's Gorton locomotive works in Manchester. *Dot*, a 0-4-0ST built in 1887 by the company for use on this system, has been preserved. Smaller, hand-worked systems were to be found at other railway works, including the LNWR's carriage works at Wolverton, where until 1926 a 3ft 6in tramway also ran from the works to Stony Stratford.

To Fort Augustus
Spean Bridge
Tulloch
To Mallaig
Lochaber Smelter
Loch Treig
Fort William
Ben Nevis
To Glasgow

Water lines

Leeds and Harrogate are just two examples where former water boards used narrow-gauge railways at their works. Narrow-gauge railways were also used in the 1920s for the construction of some reservoirs. At Elslack and Scout Dike in Yorkshire, 3ft-gauge lines were used, while at Burnhope in County Durham and at Trentabank in Cheshire there were 2ft-gauge lines.

The longest line was the 22-mile, 3ft-gauge railway that ran from Fort William to a new dam that was being constructed at Loch Treig. Opened in 1925, the Lochaber Upper Works Railway crossed a particularly rugged part of the Scottish Highlands, reaching a height of 1,120ft, before descending to Loch Treig. The railway was used to convey materials to the dam and to service a water-pipe that connected the dam with the

Above:
Stable companions: Horwich Works narrow-gauge Ruston shunter ZM32 and *Wren*, which was still used as a standby when the diesel underwent repairs. This view was taken at Horwich on 4 March 1961. The diesel also survived into preservation. *I. Holt*

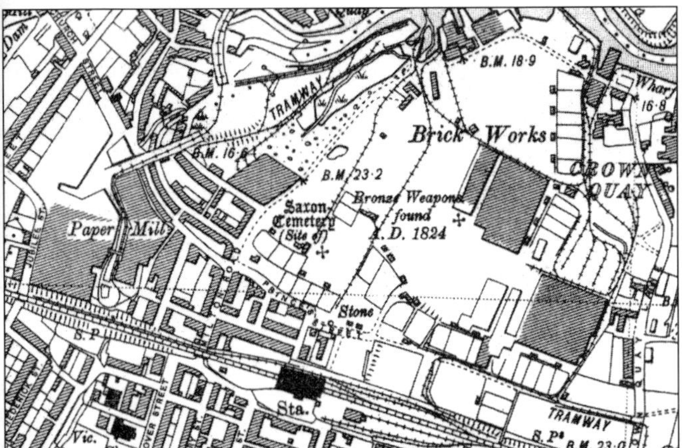

Above: A four-wheel petrol locomotive and a flat truck improvising as a passenger vehicle are seen here on 30 March 1962. They are stopped at bridge No 8 on the snow-covered hillside above Roy Bridge in Scotland, on the 22-mile 3ft-gauge Lochaber Upper Works Railway. *Hugh Davies*

Left: Sittingbourne Mill and Milton Creek area in 1938. *Crown copyright*

Below: Sunbury, one of three Kerr Stuart 0-4-2T locomotives supplied to the Metropolitan Water Board. It is seen here at Sunbury pumping station. The 3½-mile, 2ft-gauge line opened in 1915, and linked the Thames at Hampton with works at Sunbury and Kempton Park. It closed in 1947. *LPC*

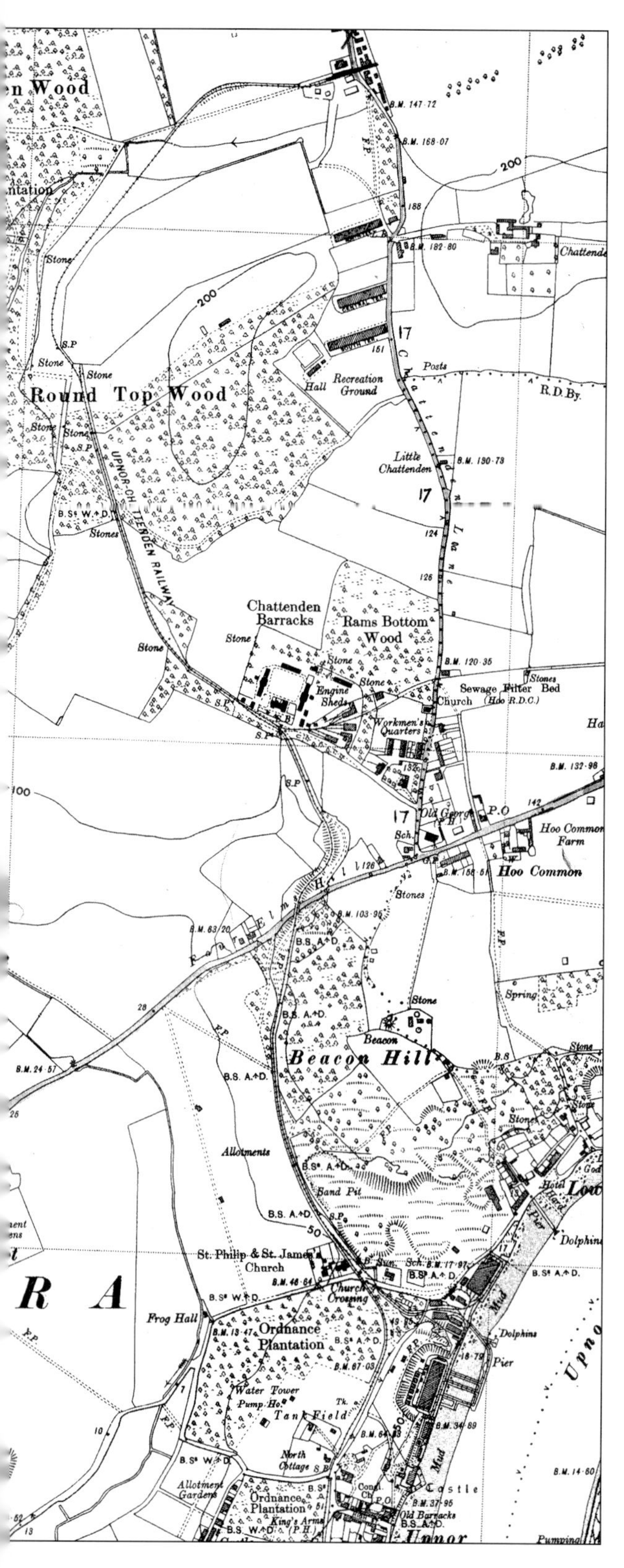

Lochaber aluminium works. Although originally intended as a temporary construction railway, it was decided to retain the line for maintenance purposes. Two locomotives and a number of battery engines were used, and both freight and passenger services for workmen developed. In 1969 floods damaged sections of the route, and it was decided to run the railway down, with the line finally closing in 1977.

Mills and hills

There were once many narrow-gauge lines in north Kent. The growth of the paper industry at Sittingbourne led to the development of a 2ft 6in-gauge railway system, opened in 1906 from Milton Creek to the Sittingbourne mills. The wharves at Milton Creek were prone to silting up, and by 1914 the narrow-gauge line had been extended to new docks at Ridham. In 1924 a paper-mill was built at Kemsley and workmen's trains were run on the railway, with some services operating during the early hours of the morning.

A busy system developed, and by the mid-1950s over a dozen steam locomotives could be seen in operation. The largest, *Monarch*, dating from 1953, was one of the last steam locomotives built for a British industrial narrow-gauge railway. Such was the importance of the system that a temporary route to the coast, at Burley Wharf, was constructed after the East Coast floods of 1953 put the docks at Ridham out of use.

In 1969 it was decided to close the system, and the extension to Ridham Docks, together with the high-level line into the works at Sittingbourne, are no more. Yet this was not to be the end of the railway. To the credit of the Bowater Company, a 2-mile central section was retained and is run by the Sittingbourne & Kemsley Light Railway.

Passengers are now carried through an industrial landscape, often in 'toastrack' coaches from the former Chattenden & Upnor Railway. This nearby military railway served an ammunition depot at Lodge Hill and Chattenden Barracks. The line skirted round Beacon Hill to reach wharves at Upnor on the River Medway. Originally built to standard gauge, the line was converted to 2ft 6in gauge by the Royal Engineers at the turn of the last century.

The Chattenden & Upnor Railway was taken over by the Admiralty in 1906. Army and Navy personnel, together with freight in the form of armaments from the Woolwich Arsenal, used the line. The railway was modernised and restocked during and after World War 2, but closed in 1961. Short sections of the disused railway remain visible in the landscape, whilst other sections have been converted into roadways. Some of the stock has also been preserved.

Left: Route of the Chattenden & Upnor Railway in 1938. *Crown copyright*

Above: By 1911 a double-track 3ft-gauge line had been opened between Loch Leven and the British Aluminium smelter at Kinlochleven. Hydro-electricity provided the power. One of the three four-wheel overhead-supply electric locomotives is seen on the quayside in September 1958. The railway closed in 1960. *David Lawrence*

Below: Complete with distinctive spark-arrester chimney, *Excelsior*, a Kerr Stuart 0-4-2ST enters the paper-mill at Sittingbourne on 16 November 1963. The metal viaduct that led from the holding yard to the mill is no longer used by trains, but a central section of the railway has been preserved and remains in use. *Ian Allan Library*

Above: The Chattenden & Upnor Railway Officers' Saloon coach, followed by one of the more basic semi-open 'toastrack' coaches used on the former Admiralty line. They are seen here on Welshpool & Llanfair Railway, before the 'toastrack' coaches were returned to Kent for use on the Sittingbourne & Kemsley Light Railway. *P. Sharpe*

Below: Chattenden, a six-coupled diesel built by the Drewry Car Co at Burton-upon-Trent in 1949 for the 2ft 6in-gauge military Chattenden & Upnor Railway. The line closed in 1961, and the locomotive is seen here at Llanfair, on the Welshpool & Llanfair Light Railway, in June 1999. *Author*

21 The Royal Arsenal Railway

Narrow-gauge systems were widely used during World War 1. The War Department ran some 745 miles of narrow-gauge railway and utilised 663 60cm-gauge locomotives in France, together with over 1,000 petrol engines and tractors. After the war, the surplus stock enabled existing lines to restock and new lines to be built relatively cheaply. During World War 2 little use was made of narrow-gauge lines as a direct means of warfare, but narrow-gauge railways continued in use at a number of military support establishments.

One of the most famous military establishments was the Royal Arsenal at Woolwich, founded in 1805 to produce armaments. An early tramway system existed at the Arsenal from the 1820s; by the 1860s this had developed into a 1ft 6in-gauge system serving some of the key buildings. The first steam engine was delivered to the site in 1871 and the railway opened officially in 1873.

By the 1900s about 400 wagons daily were using the system, which comprised over 30 miles of narrow-gauge track and 25 miles of mixed-gauge track. It eventually connected the main buildings with the South Eastern Railway to wharves on the River Thames and to a canal that ran into the site. The Royal Arsenal Railway developed a circular network of lines that minimised the need for train reversals; branches ran off the circular route, and numerous wagon turntables and sharp bends, facilitated by the 1ft 6in gauge, enabled the railway to serve flexibly all parts of the site.

Expansion continued, and the extent of eventual lines meant that the railway was run in six sections. During World War 1, over 100 miles of narrow-gauge track could entail over 60 locomotives being in use at any one time. Passenger services were also run for the staff within the site, with trains running at regular intervals and stopping every ¼ mile. First-, second- and third-class accommodation was provided on the trains.

The fear of fire was always present. Wagons were provided with zinc fireproof roofs and those painted red indicated that they were conveying hazardous loads. Coal-burning locomotives were provided with spark-arresters, and crews had to observe strict operating rules. Oil-burning steam engines and (later) diesels all helped to keep fire risks to a minimum.

After World War 1 the production of armaments decreased, and the 1920s saw a decline in the system. By 1922 only 10 steam locomotives remained and passenger trains were all third class; in 1933 the first of 400 items of rolling stock were offered for sale. Nevertheless, during World War 2 several diesel locomotives were purchased for use on the system. The decline of Britain as a world power in the 1950s saw the railway become less frequently used. 1960 saw the end of steam and the Arsenal itself closed in 1967, when most of the remaining stock was disposed of, although some of the wagons were not finally removed from the site until 1990.

Today, very little evidence of the railway remains on the site, but some of the former stock has been preserved, including one of the original steam locomotives.

Right: Royal Arsenal Railway 0-4-0ST No 269 *Culverin*, built in 1884 by Hudswell Clarke with an enclosed cab. It is seen c1920 coupled to one of the Superintendent Saloon coaches, RAR 77, with standard-gauge tracks in the foreground, within the Royal Arsenal site at Woolwich.
Ian Allan Library

Left: Hannibal, a 0-4-0ST built by Hudswell Clarke in 1885, is seen here within the Royal Arsenal after World War 1. The bulge at the base of the chimney is a Neath spark-arrester. Every effort was made to prevent fire spreading from the engines, and particularly strict rules applied to steam-locomotive operation on the site. *Ian Allan Library*

Centre left: A more conventional spark-arrester is seen on *Sheffield*, a coal-fired Avonside 0-4-0T, heading a four-coach internal passenger train. The headboard proclaims '17 Passenger Train No 1'; with up to 60 trains in use on the system, at its peak, train and route identification was necessary. Note the two low-hung, Woolwich-built coaches, leading. *Ian Allan Library*

Below left: Clearly the lower working ranks at the Arsenal did not travel in much luxury. This 'knifeboard' third-class open coach, RAR 774, seen here in the 1920s, was unbraked, unsprung and uncovered, thus providing a rather basic passenger facility. *Ian Allan Library*

Right: Charlton, a Bristol-built Avonside 0-4-0T dating from 1916, with a headboard proclaiming '23 Coaling No 2'. Unlike a number of oil-burning locomotives used on the 1ft 6in narrow-gauge railway, this engine was coal-fired. There were 16 locomotives of this type provided for the railway. *Ian Allan Library*

Centre right: Some items of rolling stock from the Royal Arsenal Railway survive. This was one of the larger eight-wheeled covered bogie wagons used on the system. The van was painted red, to denote that it was conveying explosive material. It is seen here in June 1999, on a length of original cast-iron tram plate at the North Woolwich Museum. *Author*

Below right: 0-4-0T engine *Woolwich* was built in 1916 by Avonside, and was the only steam locomotive to survive — together with two diesel locomotives — from the Royal Arsenal Railway. The steam engine is seen here in use on the Bicton Woodland Railway, prior to the latter's conversion to a miniature line. *Ivo Peters*

22 Wiping the slate

North Wales is renowned for the quality of its slate. The Industrial Revolution created a huge demand for roofing, and production peaked in the 1860s and 1870s. After this period there was a decline in the industry, and from World War 2 the decline accelerated. About 10 tons of waste is produced for every ton of finished slate, and consequently the scars of the slate industry remain clearly visible in many parts of Wales.

The location of this mineral wealth, combined with the mountainous terrain, resulted in more narrow-gauge railways being constructed in this part of Wales than anywhere else in Britain. As such, the history of narrow-gauge railways in the area is complex, lines being opened and closed and gauges being changed throughout the duration of major slate-working in the area. Poor track conditions at the quarries led to gauge variations, and double-flanged wheels, independently capable of sliding along their axles, were used at some locations.

Blaenau Ffestiniog

An extensive slate-quarrying area was centred on Blaenau Ffestiniog. As the slate seam ran at an angle, not all lines were on the surface. Over 20 miles of narrow-gauge underground tramways once ran in vast labyrinths of man-made slate caverns. The Festiniog Railway served the area and allowed slate trains to reach the coast by gravity.

Other slate operations also led to railway construction, and numerous tramways and railways

Below: One of the inclines connecting Duffws station with the slate quarries in the area. This scene dates from 13 May 1949, after closure of the Festiniog Railway. Abandoned rolling stock can be seen in the foreground, but at this time slate quarries still used part of the line to connect with the standard-gauge freight yards at Blaenau Ffestiniog. *D. Callender*

once existed in the area. The Croesor Tramway opened in 1864 to a 2ft gauge, and later a section became part of the route of the Welsh Highland Railway. The Festiniog & Blaenau Railway opened in 1868, but in 1883 was converted, by the GWR, to standard gauge as part of the Bala branch.

An entry in my diary for 1964 reports several hundred narrow-gauge slate wagons at Blaenau Ffestiniog station. Today there are none, but an extensive amount of industrial and railway archaeology remains and there is a museum at the Llechwedd slate caverns.

Above right: A Wingrove & Rogers four-wheeled battery-electric locomotive of 1ft 11½in gauge, with an ex-Festiniog Railway slate wagon at the Llechwedd slate mines near Blaenau Ffestiniog on 22 June 1976. A similar battery locomotive and a number of Festiniog Railway slate wagons have been preserved at the slate museum at Llechwedd. *K. Lane*

Right: The Eclipse, a 1ft 11½in-gauge electric locomotive, at Llechwedd slate mines in 1976. This locomotive was originally a Bagnall steam saddle-tank locomotive built in 1895, and was rebuilt as an electric in 1927. Two of these unusual machines are preserved at the slate museum at Llechwedd. *E. Ruffell*

Penrhyn

The slate at Penrhyn was found on the open mountainside. Prior to the use of railways, over 400 packhorses were employed in conveying the slate to the coast. The 1ft 11in-gauge, 6-mile Penrhyn Railway is generally regarded as one of the first major slate lines to open, in 1801. The route that was originally constructed descended by inclines from over 550ft at the slate quarries, near Bethesda, to the harbour at Port Penrhyn. Between 1874 and 1876 the line was realigned to use steam power. A passenger service was provided for quarrymen until 1951.

Remaining slate traffic on the line declined, and the Penrhyn Railway ceased to be used after the summer of 1962, although the quarry continued production. The locomotives *Blanche* and *Linda* found their way to the Festiniog Railway. My diary reports of torn-up tracks in 1964, but other remains of the railway, including a third locomotive used on the line, *Charles*, are to be found at Penrhyn Castle.

Left: Charles, a Hunslet 0-4-0ST dating from 1882, heads a quarrymen's train on the 1ft 10¾in-gauge Penrhyn Railway, near Tregath in July 1940. Workmen are alighting from the four-wheeled unsprung and unbraked open coaches before the train has stopped. There were at one time 16 such coaches. *W. Garth*

Centre left: Linda, a Hunslet 0-4-0ST dating from 1893, passes Felin Hen on the Penrhyn Railway, on the way to the quarries. Prior to closure of the line in 1962, *Linda* was transferred, on indefinite hire, to the Festiniog Railway. *Ivo Peters*

Below left: Blanche, a Hunslet 0-4-0ST locomotive dating from 1893 and seen here shunting at Port Penrhyn on 27 June 1956. On closure of the line in 1963, *Blanche* was to join her sister *Linda* on the Festiniog Railway. *R. Vincent*

Above: A two-horse-power slate train seen at Nantlle. This 3ft 6in-gauge horse-operated line became one of the more unusual and antiquated sections of BR prior to its closure in 1963. *SLS*

Right: A Nantlle slate wagon dating from 1828 and seen here preserved at Tywyn in June 1999. The double-flanged wheels were capable of sliding along their axles in order to run on roughly-gauged track, but this resulted in complex points arrangements. *Author*

Nantlle

At Nantlle, slate was obtained by an open-pit method, and some of the pits reached huge proportions. In order to compete with other slate producers in the area, the various quarries co-operated to open the Nantlle Railway in 1828. The 9¼-mile, 3ft 6in-gauge line ran from quarries in the Nantlle area to quays at Caernarfon. Passengers were conveyed between 1856 and 1865.

By 1867 the section of the narrow-gauge line between Pen-y-Groes and Caernarfon had become part of the Carnarvonshire Railway and had been converted to standard gauge, and by 1872 a further section of line, to Nantlle, had been similarly converted. The Carnarvonshire Railway was absorbed by the LNWR and later became part of the LMS; thus, in due course, the remaining horse-worked narrow-gauge lines, to a number of local slate-producing areas in the Nantlle area, became a unique part of British Railways. They were not closed until 1963 and, even then, a number of short quarry lines survived for a few more years.

Above: A two-horse train of narrow-gauge wagons has just arrived on the raised trans-shipment wharf at Nantlle standard-gauge station. In this view, taken in 1957, the train was hauled by BR horses *Prince* and *Queen*. *David Lawrence*

Above: No 1 *Rough Pup*, a 1ft 10¾ in-gauge Hunslet locomotive dating from 1891. It is pictured here for the last time at the Dinorwic quarries, where it spent the whole of its working life, prior to its preservation. In spite of frequently wet conditions, no cab was provided. This was in order to keep the weight of the locomotive to a minimum and to allow maximum flexibility on the narrow slate galleries. *R. Palk*

Opposite: A cartographic nightmare! The rock formations and lines of the Dinorwic quarry in 1920. *Crown copyright*

Dinorwic

At Dinorwic, slate was also obtained from the open mountainside. A horse-operated narrow-gauge line opened in 1824, linking the quarries near Llanberis with Port Dinorwic. In 1848 a new 7-mile section of line to the coast was built to a 4ft gauge and became known as the Padarn Railway. Replacing the earlier route, the new steam-operated line was able to convey two of the smaller 1ft 10¾ in-gauge quarry trucks, side by side, on transporter wagons.

In terms of the scale of the operation, over 2,000 wagons were once used on 50 miles of narrow-gauge line at the quarry itself. The Padarn Railway also provided a service for quarrymen; at its peak, the quarry employed 15,000, and a 20-coach train was required, but by World War 2 trains required only two or three coaches, and services ended in 1947. The railway closed in October 1961, and my diary records ripped-up track at Port Dinorwic in 1964. The remaining Dinorwic quarry railways closed in November 1967, ending the pure slate lines in North Wales.

Many of the small Hunslet quarry locomotives were dispersed for preservation. A section of the Padarn Railway is now used by the 1ft 11½ in-gauge Llanberis Lake Railway, while the former quarry workshops at Llanberis have become part of the Welsh Slate Museum.

Elidir Fâch
Post Office
Aelwyd-uchaf
Tan-y-marian
Rises
Tan-y-garret
Bryn-goleu
Ty-Dilew
Pant Sardis
Dinorwic
Reservoir
Sheepfold
Afon Fachwen
Tank
Trial Level
Incline
Pile of Stones
2564
Stones
Allt-ddu
Allt-ddu Slate Quarry
Tanks
Tunnel
Garret
Bryn-llys
Sheepfold
Elidir View
Rises
Afon Dervyn
Bron-Elidir
Bron-fuches
Rhen-hospital
Hafotty
Tank
Braich
Dinorwic Slate Quarries
Sheepfold
Old Incline
Tunnels
Matilda
Wellington
Victoria
Sheepfold
LLYN PERIS
Cwm-aelhir-isaf
Surface of Water
339·5
29th. September 1886.
Sheep Shelter
Gareg-wen
Cwm-aelhir

Left: Dinorwic, a powerful Hunslet 0-6-0T engine, was introduced on the 4ft-gauge Padarn Railway in 1882. Two sister locomotives followed, operating the line until 1961, after which the engines were scrapped and all the coaches, except one, burned. *R. Vincent*

Below: One of the slate-carrying, cable-operated inclines at Dinorwic, seen here in September 1999. Most inclines at the quarry were gravity-acting, and connected the different slate galleries to lower levels and the Padarn Railway.
Author's collection

Below: Double-wagon turntables, of the flat-iron-disc type, preserved at the Welsh Slate Museum at Llanberis. Wagons were turned by hand, and the funnel arrangements guided the double-flanged slate-truck wheels back onto the rails.
Author's collection

23 Remains of the clay

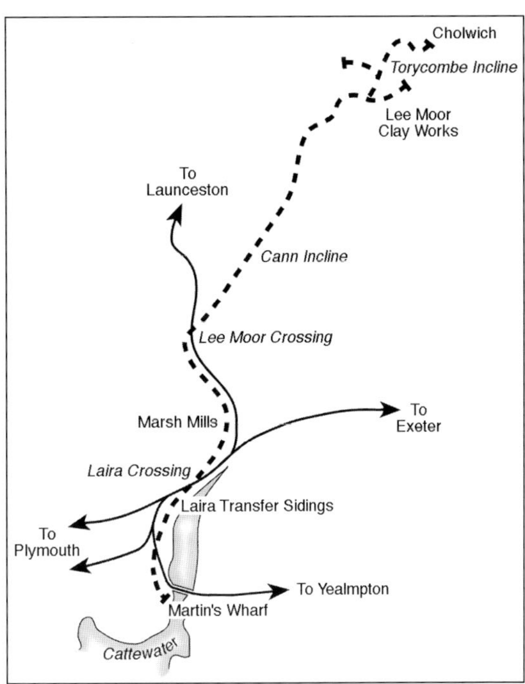

Left: The Torycombe incline winding-drum, showing the counter-balancing brake controlling the speed of trucks on the incline, the descending train being heavier than the ascending. The beam supported the drumhouse floor at rail level. The incline was last used in 1936; this view was taken in the early 1960s before the line was more fully dismantled.
Ian Allan Library

Mineral railways developed in every part of Britain where minerals of any kind were to be found in any quantity. A number of narrow-gauge railways were constructed to transport clay. In the South West, the 3ft-gauge Marland Railway ran in the Torridge Valley. At nearby Meeth there was once a 2ft system, and the 2ft 6in Pentewan Railway closed in 1918. Clay-carrying lines could also be found elsewhere, and were built to an equally bewildering variety of narrow gauges.

Dartmoor crossings

The Lee Moor Tramway, at 4ft 6in, is almost of standard gauge, but is worthy of mention. This was a privately-owned tramway built to convey china clay from the Lee Moor quarries, on the southwest slopes of Dartmoor, to Martin's Wharf at Plymouth. The majority of the line was constructed in 1853, but, because of building defects, considerable improvements were necessary before the official opening in 1858. The 7½-mile route descended from a height of 750ft at Lee Moor, by inclines and horse-worked sections. In 1899 steam traction was introduced on the Torycombe to Cann Wood part of the route, but other sections remained horse-operated until final closure.

The remote section from Lee Moor to Cholwich closed in 1910, followed by the Torycombe incline in 1936. Much of the remaining tramway closed to regular traffic in 1939, yet occasional trains continued to use the lower parts of the line. The tramway included level rail crossings with the lines to Launceston and Cattewater. However, the level rail crossing of the four-track GWR main line at Laira, outside Plymouth, which operated right up until 1960, was the most unique aspect of the tramway. Parts of the route are still evident, and both locomotives and a wagon that once operated on the line have been preserved.

Above: The single-line Lee Moor tramway crossed the GWR main line on the level at Laira, to the east of Plymouth, right up until 1960. A gate protected the four main railway lines, as can be seen in this view taken after closure of the tramway. The last train to cross the main line did so in August 1960, and the crossing was removed in the autumn of that year. *Ian Allan Library*

Left: Whitegates level crossing, on the Yelverton to Plymouth road on the Torycombe side on the Lee Moor Tramway, after regular use of the 4ft 6in-gauge line had ceased in 1960. *Ian Allan Library*

Isle of Purbeck

A number of narrow-gauge lines were once used to transport clay on the Isle of Purbeck. The firm of Pike Bros, Fayle & Co operated two narrow-gauge systems in the area. The Furzebrook (or Pike's) Tramway, as it was known, was a 2ft 8½in system that opened in 1840. The line transported the fine, white firing-clay from pits near Furzebrook and Creech to Ridge Wharf on the River Frome. The tramway became steam-operated from 1866 and a network of lines developed.

During World War 2, raids on coastal shipping led to the line being cut back to an interchange on the Swanage branch at Furzebrook. In 1953 a short section of new line was constructed, and three locomotives were regularly in steam at this time. Nevertheless, the entire system had ceased operation by the mid-1960s. Today several parts of the route are used as roadways.

The other railway operated by the company was at one time a 3ft 9in-gauge line that ran from clay works at Norden to Goathorn pier, on the southern side of Poole Harbour. World War 2 also resulted in this line being cut back to the relative safety of the Swanage branch at Norden. By 1947 the original locomotives were worn out, and it was decided to re-lay the line to a 2ft gauge using second-hand stock that included, for a time, the former Welsh Highland Railway locomotive *Russell*. The short remaining section was the last narrow-gauge line in the area to close, lasting until 1971.

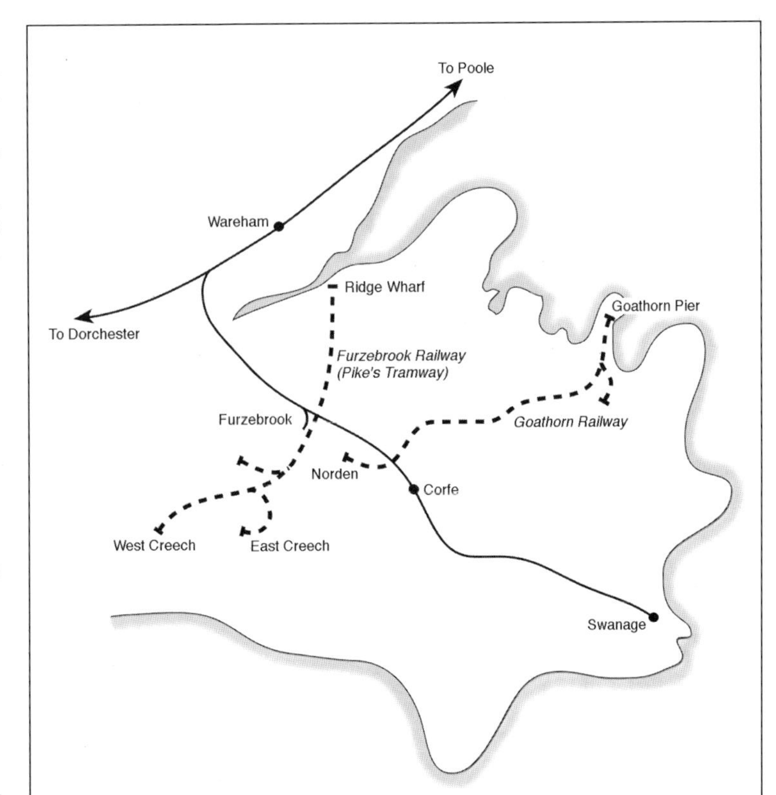

Below: Quintus, a Manning Wardle 0-4-0ST built in 1914 and pictured in woodland near Creech Grange on the Pike Bros, Fayle & Co clay-carrying Furzebrook Railway, in August 1954. Although the railway is no more, some former sections of line have been converted for use as roadways. *Ivo Peters*

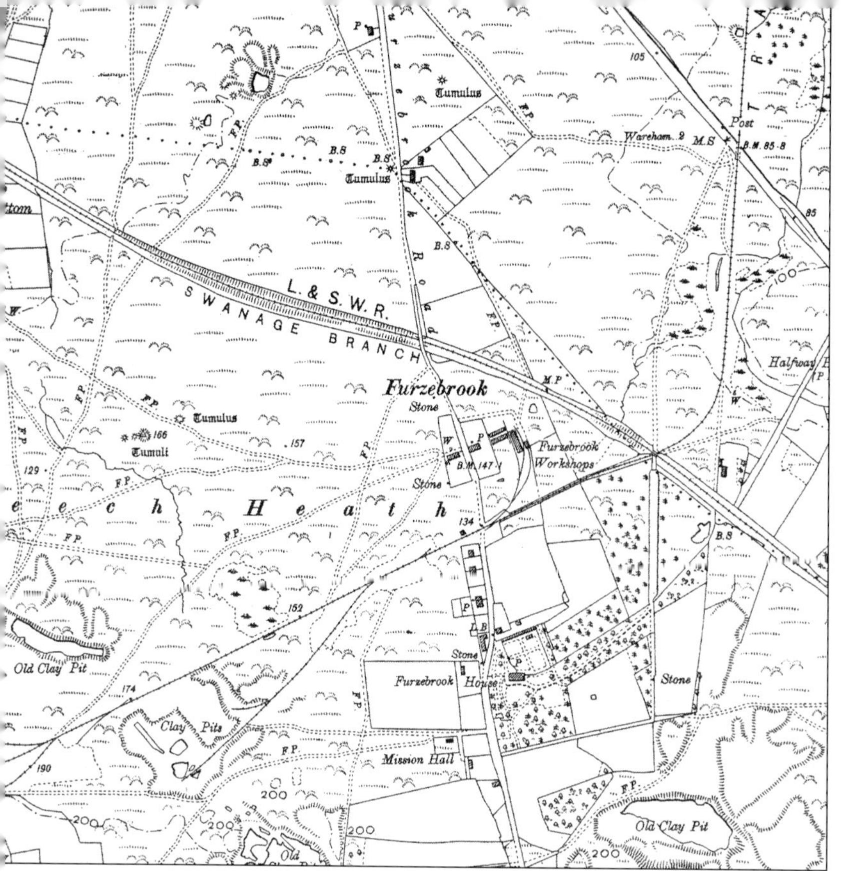

Left: The fine white firing-clay found on the Isle of Purbeck resulted in narrow-gauge lines being constructed in the area. The first tramway, built by the firm of Pike, dates back to about 1840. This map shows lines in the Furzebrook area in 1902. *Crown copyright*

Below: Secundus was built by Seekings in 1874. The 0-6-0WT is seen outside the shed at Furzebrook on the 2ft 8in-gauge Furzebrook Railway, on 31 May 1955. It was subsequently preserved. *R. Stieber*

Right: Thames, a Manning Wardle 0-4-0ST built in 1902 and owned by Pike Bros, Fayle & Co, at the clay-pits near Corfe Castle on the Goathorn Railway, on 26 August 1948. At this time, the line was of 3ft 9in gauge. *D. Box*

Centre right: Russell in a derelict state near Corfe, on the Goathorn Railway, in 1955. The railway was converted from 3ft 9in gauge to 2ft gauge to accommodate second-hand stock, which included *Russell*, a 2-6-2T from the Welsh Highland Railway. *Russell* fortunately survived. *R. Holmes*

Bottom left: The Goathorn Railway at Norden, with an Orenstein & Koppel-built four-wheel diesel locomotive at the Mines Depot in July 1956. The line crossed the main A351 road at Norden, north-west of Swanage, on the level. Closure of this remaining section came in 1971. *W. Davies*

Bottom right: An old engine shed at Ridge Wharf, near Wareham, still endures, as this view taken in August 1999 shows. Other remains of the clay-carrying railways can also be found on the Isle of Purbeck. *Author*

Left: London Brick Co electric transfer locomotive No 6, seen here in September 1937. A notice informs that riding on the locomotive is prohibited. The heavy load of Fletton bricks being conveyed has been taken out of one of the brick-kilns. By 1936 the company's brickworks at Stewartby was producing 500 million bricks per year. *Ian Allan Library*

Below left: Two London Brick Co locomotives at Stewartby, which was the largest brickworks in the world. A series of 2ft 11in-gauge railways once served the works and clay-pits. S1, to the right, dates from 1929 and S3, on the left, dates from 1935. The casing enclosing the chain drive was a distinctive feature of these Sentinel narrow-gauge steam locomotives. *SLS*

Marston Vale

During the 19th century bricks became pre-eminent as a major form of construction and local brickworks developed in all parts of the country where suitable clay could be found. Narrow-gauge railways were a feature of many works.

The development of the main-line railway network provided wider access to markets for bricks. This made areas such as Bedfordshire, which had substantial exposures of suitable clay in the Marston Vale, ideal for brick-making. Vast brickworks developed, employing a variety of narrow-gauge systems.

At Stewartby the incline railway from the clay-pit was of 2ft 11in gauge, each wagon having a capacity of 5 tons. At Elstow the incline railway was of 2ft gauge and here each wagon had a capacity of less than 2 tons. In each case an electric motor operated chains hauling full wagons to the works and returning empties to the clay-pit. The Stewartby railway system was abandoned in 1953, and that at Elstow in 1962.

Where the brickworks were further away from clay-pits, a 2ft 6in-gauge line was installed at the Coronation Works near Stewartby and a 2ft 5½in-gauge line at Ridgemont. These lines were later converted to cable operation, the Coronation system closing when the works closed in 1974, and the Ridgemont system being converted to a conveyor-belt in 1978.

24 Field and furnace

Almost all narrow-gauge mineral railways have succumbed to other forms of transport. Yet losses are not a recent phenomenon, as mineral deposits, once exhausted, led to the inevitable closure of the supporting narrow-gauge systems. There are recorded closures of mineral wagonways from the 1700s. Some narrow-gauge lines lasted for many years, but others, such as the 2ft 3in Hafan & Talybont Tramway in 1898, closed after just about a year of operation.

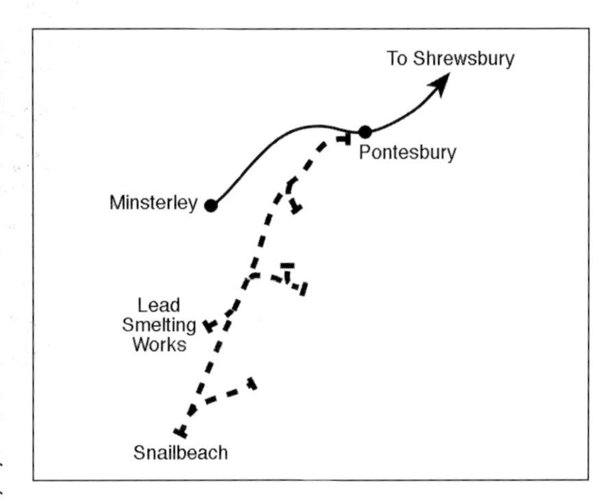

Snailbeach

The Snailbeach District Railways served lead mines and a smelting works in Shropshire, and ran from Pontesbury, on the GWR and LNWR joint line, to the Stiperstones Hills. The 2ft 3¾ in-gauge line reached Snailbeach in 1877, but plans to extend to a number of other lead mines in the area never proceeded. It is of interest that the Glyn Valley Tramway was almost of the same gauge, and locomotives were transferred between the two systems.

Closure of the Snailbeach line came in 1915. Yet the resourceful Colonel Stephens took over in 1923 and reopened the line to serve quarries on the route. He even considered operating passenger services, but nothing came of this idea. Although freight traffic was limited, the Snailbeach line utilised second-hand stock and continued in a run-down and *ad hoc* way until 1959, when the remaining northern section of line was closed. Following closure, the Talyllyn Railway purchased some of the rails. Today, remains are still to be found and it is possible to walk along much of the old route.

Below: Snailbeach locomotive shed, with Snailbeach District Railways Nos 2 and 4 seen outside in 1925. The remains of *Dennis*, a Bagnall 0-6-0T dating from 1910, can also be seen on the right; this was the only original locomotive to remain after Colonel Stephens took over. An overhaul was never completed and *Dennis*, along with all the other engines, was eventually scrapped. *Ian Allan Library*

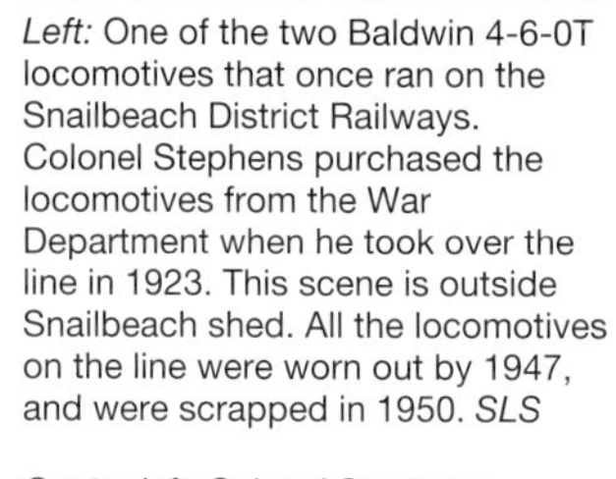

Left: One of the two Baldwin 4-6-0T locomotives that once ran on the Snailbeach District Railways. Colonel Stephens purchased the locomotives from the War Department when he took over the line in 1923. This scene is outside Snailbeach shed. All the locomotives on the line were worn out by 1947, and were scrapped in 1950. *SLS*

Centre left: Colonel Stephens purchased No 2, a Kerr Stuart 0-4-2T, second-hand from the Admiralty in 1923 for use on the Snailbeach line. A boiler problem resulted in the locomotive being unusable by 1946 and it was eventually scrapped in 1950. *SLS*

Below: The interchange ramp at Pontesbury main-line station in about 1925 — note the precarious state of the walkway. During the final years of the railway, wagons were conveyed along the line by a farm tractor. *Ian Allan Library*

Nocton

There were once narrow-gauge freight systems associated with agriculture, and a number of railways developed in Lincolnshire to transport potatoes, in particular. One of the most noteworthy was the 24-mile 2ft (60cm)-gauge system of the Nocton Potato Estates. The main line followed the field boundaries on the flat Nocton Fen and helped to provide a link from Dunston & Nocton station, on the Great Northern & Great Eastern Joint Committee line, to Bardney Junction on the Great Northern Railway. The Nocton railway utilised redundant World War 1 track and stock, mainly from the Arras area of France.

On closure, some of the track and stock was again reused in 1960 to establish the Lincolnshire Coast Light Railway, near Cleethorpes. This 1-mile tourist line also acquired stock from the Sand Hutton and Ashover lines, but was subsequently closed.

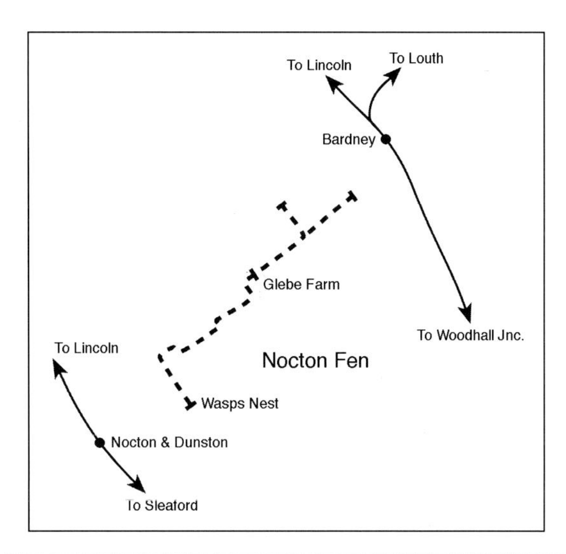

Above right: The Nocton Railway's No 7, dating from 1920, can be seen in the shed, while *Elin*, a 0-4-0ST from Penrhyn, and a Simplex are also present at South Sea Lane, on the former Lincolnshire Coast Light Railway. The 2ft-gauge railway was opened in 1960, using equipment from the former Nocton Railway, but was subsequently closed. This view was taken on 20 July 1985. *R. Ruffell*

Right: Jurassic, a Peckett-built 0-6-0ST which came from the cement works at Southam in Warwickshire, waits at the North Sea terminus of the Lincolnshire Coast Light Railway. The coach originates from the Ashover Light Railway. *W. Davies*

Kettering

Iron played a prominent part in Britain's Industrial Revolution, and the Kettering ironstone fields owed their development to the railways. The Kettering Iron & Coal Co was established in 1871 and a network of 3ft-gauge lines developed from the orefields to the furnaces at Kettering. The furnaces were built in 1878 and were located to the north of the town, adjoining the Midland main line. From 1879 steam worked the ever-expanding and -changing network of narrow-gauge lines.

Kettering was the oldest significant ironstone system, and during its heyday the operation could involve a dozen locomotives. As individual orefields became exhausted, lines were dismantled, and the first closures on the system date from the 1890s. The lack of transhipment in reaching the furnaces sustained the railway's long existence, but the Kettering furnaces closed in 1959 and the railway followed in 1962. Restoration of the orefields to agriculture, and an industrial estate in the area of the furnaces, have resulted in there being few physical remains today.

Narrow-gauge ironstone railways could be found at a number of other locations such as Islip, Eastwell, Scaldwell and Eaton. These systems were mainly closed in the 1950s, while the 3ft-gauge lines at Wellingborough lasted until 1966.

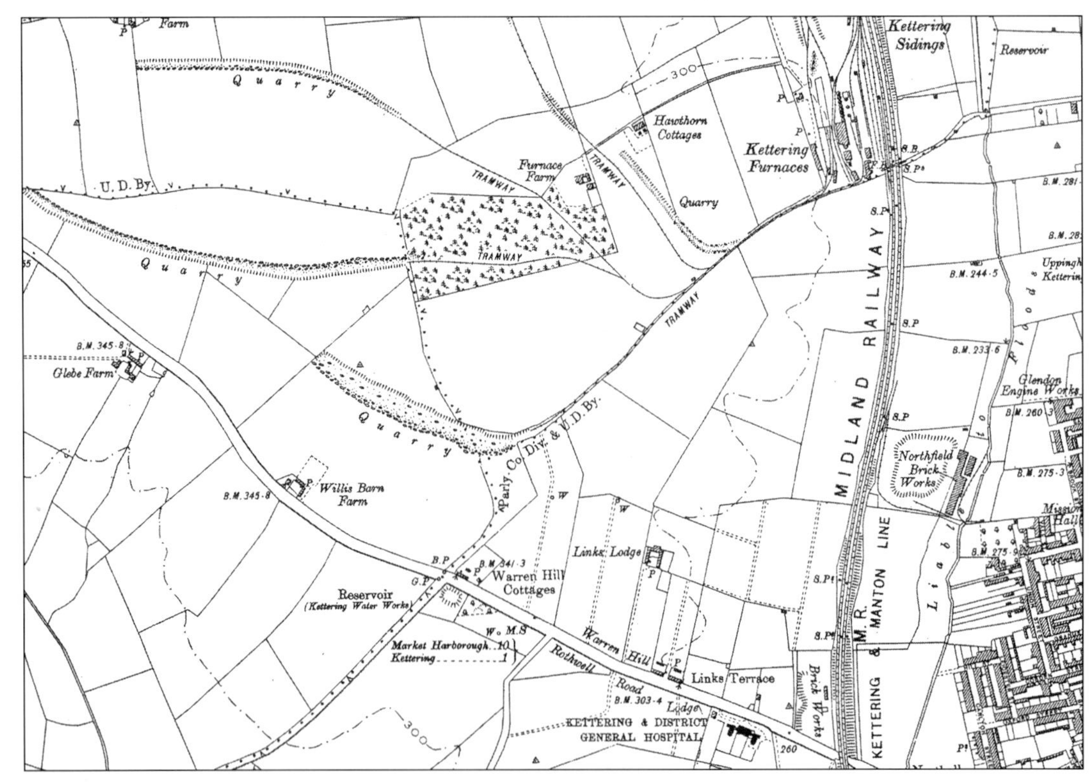

Left: Manning Wardle *Kettering Furnaces No 7* waits alongside *Kettering Furnaces No 2*, a Black Hawthorn 0-4-0ST of 3ft gauge dating from 1885, in August 1961; both locomotives belonged to the Kettering Iron & Coal Co Ltd. Note the full- and half-size cabs. *G. King*

Below left: The Kettering furnaces and nearby ironstone quarries in 1910. *Crown copyright*

Right: Manning Wardle 0-6-0ST *Kettering Furnaces No 7* with a passenger special to celebrate 10 years of The Narrow Gauge Railway Society. The train is seen at one of the surface ironstone workings in 1961. The quarry system closed the following year. *G. Lumb*

Centre right: Manning Wardle 0-6-0ST *Kettering Furnaces No 6* heads a train of iron ore from the quarry at Rothwell. *Kettering Furnaces No 7* waits in the background to propel the wagons into the tipping stage. *Kettering Furnaces No 3* has been preserved. *G. King*

Below right: Wellingborough Ironstone Quarries also operated a 3ft-gauge system. Here No 85, a Peckett 0-6-0ST, leaves the quarry with a loaded train of ore on 2 June 1966, in the last year of operation. Dating from 1934, the locomotive was subsequently preserved at Irchester. *P. Groom*

Black Diamond

Coal was the mineral that resulted in the greatest cumulative amount of lost narrow-gauge railway in Britain. At one time almost everything was dependent on coal, including the power for nearly every line mentioned in this book. Such was its importance that coal was known as the 'Black Diamond'. However, the 1920s witnessed the onset of a prolonged decline in the coal industry, with South Wales being particularly hard-hit.

There are several methods of coal extraction and until the 1960s there were still over 2,000 collieries in Britain. Narrow-gauge lines could be found at many of these collieries. Coal would travel underground to the pit-head, and often to the standard-gauge interchange, by narrow-gauge trains of loose-coupled coal tubs.

Gas was also once made from coal, and narrow-gauge systems were used at many of the larger gasworks. In some cases up to six locomotives could be employed, serving the retort houses and extracting spent lime in a relatively complex process of gas production. By the 1960s the narrow-gauge systems had largely closed. This was followed by the gasworks themselves as natural gas was introduced.

Whole coalfields have also been abandoned, and only a handful of collieries now remains; narrow-gauge railways no longer feature in the coal-extraction operation. Nonetheless, it should be remembered that narrow-gauge wagonways can be traced back to the 1600s, and the last pit ponies to transport coal were only retired in the early 1990s. This provides evidence of about 400 years of narrow-gauge railway service to the coal industry in Britain. Few industrial technologies can claim such longevity.

Above left: Electric locomotive No 6, a Barclay-built engine dating from 1943, hauls shale on a 2ft 6in-gauge line in Scotland. At one time almost everything ran on coal, and thousands of collieries, drift and open-cast workings brought coal to the surface, or to standard-gauge interchanges, using narrow-gauge railways. *A. Vickers*

Left: No 15 *Bonnie Dundee* was a Kerr Stuart engine built in 1900 for the 2ft-gauge Dundee Corporation gasworks railway. Seen here just before withdrawal in 1959, the engine weighed a mere 3½ tons. It is now preserved in rebuilt form on the Ravenglass & Eskdale Railway. *Ian Allan Library*

Above: Dalmarnock was one of a number of Glasgow Corporation gasworks. This view shows one of the diminutive engines on the 2ft-gauge system that served the works. Dawsholm and Tradeston works also had 2ft-gauge lines, while that at Provan had a 2ft 6in-gauge system. *Ian Allan Library*

Centre right: Spartan colliery-workers' transport. These open 'knifeboard' coaches, which ran directly into drift-mines, are seen in this view at the North of England Open Air Museum, Beamish, in September 1999. *Author's collection*

Right: The last tram of coal raised in the Rhondda, seen here at a mining museum in South Wales in September 1993. Note the almost miniature scale of the subterranean narrow-gauge train and loose-coupled coal-tub. *Author's collection*

25 A living past

After years of decline and retrenchment, narrow-gauge passenger lines came to the very edge of extinction after World War 2. Yet just as modern high-speed living and the growth in road transport accelerated their decline, it also came to their rescue. Greater accessibility, holidays and wealth were the prerequisites of a growth in tourism. Equally perversely, the very lack of investment, leading to the retention of ancient steam locomotives and antiquated rolling stock, provided instant museum-pieces. Even BR assisted by banning steam and depersonalising its own lines.

Early narrow-gauge railways were constructed primarily to transport freight. Only a few still survive doing just that, for example the 2ft-gauge Post Office Railway in London. On the passenger side, the Snowdon Mountain, Great Orme, Volk's and Snaefell Mountain railways, built to exploit tourism, outlasted many others. Miniature lines have also survived; the Ravenglass & Eskdale, Fairbourne and Romney, Hythe & Dymchurch railways were built, or rebuilt, primarily for leisure use, and all remain open. Tourists saved the Vale of Rheidol when its freight sources dried up.

Other lines attempted to diversify into tourism, but not every narrow-gauge line could boast of spectacular scenery. Nevertheless, each could exploit its uniqueness. Consequently, the first major attempt at railway preservation involved a narrow-gauge line. In 1951 the Talyllyn Railway Preservation Society was set up and proved that railway enthusiasts could save and run the Talyllyn Railway. Enthusiasts went on to reopen other lines, and the railway preservation movement has done marvellous work in preventing the loss of narrow-gauge lines and in preserving equipment from those that have closed.

The Festiniog Railway closed in 1946. The Welshpool & Llanfair Railway, which was the last narrow-gauge line to operate a public freight service, closed in 1956. The Ravenglass & Eskdale Railway was put up for auction in 60 lots in 1960. The Isle of Man steam railways closed in 1965. All were saved, at least in part, by one means or another, and today losses are not nearly so extensive as once thought likely. Indeed, with projects such as the Welsh Highland, Corris and Lynton & Barnstaple, together with groups set up to support other closed lines, encouragingly there is today more chance of a narrow-gauge line reopening than closing.

Narrow-gauge lines have also been re-established all over the country. The Llanberis Lake, Leighton Buzzard (see *Lost Lines — LMR*) and Sittingbourne & Kemsley lines all provide passenger services on existing narrow-gauge railways that were once used

Left: The Snowdon Mountain Railway, with 0-4-2T No 5 *Moel Siabod*, dating from the opening of the line in 1896, at Snowdon summit station on 30 August 1926. The 2ft 7½in narrow-gauge rack railway still runs to the 3,493ft summit, the highest point of any railway in Britain. *H. C. Casserley*

primarily for freight. Elsewhere, narrow-gauge passenger lines have been constructed on former standard-gauge lost lines. In other areas, new narrow-gauge lines have been constructed where railways never previously existed. Some of the railways use equipment from closed lines, and some items of rolling stock remain from a majority of the lost passenger lines.

Not only has narrow gauge survived, but there is now an ever-increasing length of such line in use for passenger services in Britain, and more passengers are travelling on Britain's narrow-gauge railways than ever before. It is a cheering thought that narrow-gauge railways can look forward to expansion in the future, with more reopenings, new lines and new stock. Who would have foreseen this 50 years ago?

Equally, who can predict what the future will bring? With this in mind, do not leave it too long before you take that transport of delight, into a living past, on one of Britain's great little narrow-gauge railways.

Above: The great survivor. *Prince of Wales*, a 2-6-2T built in 1924, hauls a train on the Vale of Rheidol Light Railway. The train is seen leaving Aberystwyth with a 10.00am departure to Devil's Bridge in August 1960. At this time the railway was the last remaining narrow-gauge passenger line run by BR, and, although not identified for closure in the Beeching Report, faced an uncertain future. It was eventually sold to a private operator, and remains open. Reorganisation at Aberystwyth has rendered the section of line in this view redundant. *J. Haydon*

Right: No 2 *The Countess*, an 0-6-0T dating from 1902, is flagged across Church Street in Welshpool on its return from the reopening ceremony held at Llanfair on 6 April 1963. The section of line through Welshpool, between the main-line station and Raven Square, was subsequently closed in August 1963, but happily most of the former Welshpool & Llanfair Light Railway was preserved and remains in use. *Ian Allan Library*

Above: New lines for old. Having climbed to a higher level by means of the Dduallt spiral, 0-4-4-0T double Fairlie *Merddin Emrys*, dating from 1879, is seen here on the Ffestiniog Railway's deviation line, with an up train for Tanygrisiau. The disused lower line is visible on the left of the picture, taken on 10 July 1978. *R. Fisher*

Below: A train from Penllyn hauled by *Dolbadarn*, a former Dinorwic slate quarry Hunslet 0-4-0ST dating from 1922 but now with an added cab, nears Llanberis on the Llanberis Lake Railway, on 27 July 1972. The building on the right is the locomotive shed of the former 4ft-gauge Padarn Railway, on whose trackbed the Llanberis Lake Railway was constructed. *G. Gillham*

Above: A former GWR sign which provided some indication of how to reach the Welsh Highland Railway. Such directions are no longer confined to the history books, as the Welsh Highland Railway — Rheilffordd Eryri — is a living railway once again. *Author's collection*

Above right: Superb, a Bagnall 0-6-2T built in 1940, approaches Burley crossing with the 15.15 from Sittingbourne to Kemsley on 29 July 1988. The coaching stock in this view includes that from the nearby Chattenden & Upnor Railway which, until closure in 1961, ran from the River Medway to military establishments on the Hoo peninsula. *D. Gosden*

Centre right: The Leighton Buzzard Railway in Bedfordshire conveyed sand from quarries to the main line until 1977. Today, passenger trains have replaced freight. The preserved line possesses the largest collection of narrow-gauge locomotives in Britain. In this view, dating from 1971, *P. C. Allen*, a 0-4-0WT dating from 1919, receives attention during a quiet interlude. *P. Groom*

Lower right: A view of Scafell in March 1967, from the footplate of the Ravenglass & Eskdale Railway's *River Irt*. Modified from Sir Arthur Heywood's locomotive built in 1894, this 0-8-2 is the oldest working 15in-gauge locomotive in the world. The Eskdale line, in the Lake District, was almost closed for a second time in the 1960s, but was saved by railway preservationists. *C. Janaus*

Above: Isle of Man Railway 2-4-0T No 5 *Mona*, dating from 1874, enters St John's with the 2.20pm train from Douglas to Peel on Friday 5 July 1968. Although this particular section of the railway has closed, a substantial section of narrow-gauge line remains open and provides a museum on wheels on the Isle of Man. *A. Stuart*

Below: Dolgoch, a 0-4-0WT dating from 1866, hauls a mixed narrow-gauge freight train near Abergynolwyn, on the Talyllyn Railway, in September 1949. It was the pure charm of scenes like this that led to the creation of the railway preservation movement, the first being the Talyllyn. *P. B. Whitehouse*